The Rx for L.I.F.E.

The Rx for L.I.F.E.

*Spiritual medicine for your
mind, body, and soul*

365 Doses of Daily Inspiration for
Living In Faith Everyday

Dr. Malieka T. Johnson

XULON PRESS

Xulon Press
2301 Lucien Way #415
Maitland, FL 32751
407.339.4217
www.xulonpress.com

© 2018 by Dr. Malieka T. Johnson

All rights reserved solely by the author. The author guarantees all contents are original and do not infringe upon the legal rights of any other person or work. No part of this book may be reproduced in any form without the permission of the author. The views expressed in this book are not necessarily those of the publisher.

Unless otherwise indicated, Scripture quotations taken from the Holy Bible, New International Version (NIV). Copyright © 1973, 1978, 1984, 2011 by Biblica, Inc.™. Used by permission. All rights reserved.

This is a SWA:REI™ product.

Additional copies can be purchased in bulk for educational study, sales promotional use, fundraising, business, or as gifts. Please email maliekajohnson@gmail.com or write to Malieka Johnson, SWA:REI™, P.O. Box 881496 San Diego, CA 92168-1496

Printed in the United States of America.

ISBN-13: 978-1-54565-174-2

Dear Sher,
I hope this book encourages you as much as you have encouraged me. Love you & God Bless You Always

♡ Malieka

Dedication

I dedicate The Rx for L.I.F.E., a daily devotional for Living In Faith Everyday to two very important women.

To my mom, Kristi Lynn Johnson, who took the risk and challenge to bring me into the world. Thank you for your sacrifices, provisions, and continuous encouragement. I love you and appreciate you more than words can express.

To my grandmother, Margie McCraw Johnson, who continues to inspire and encourage me. Thank you for your love, support, patience, and wisdom. I love you and I am thankful for you.

Introduction

Dear Friend,

Greetings! Thank you for picking up this devotional, purchasing it, reading it, and putting it to use. This two-year passion project was an idea given to me by God that I did not think would materialize so soon. It was a far-off dream that I was happy to entertain in my thoughts, but God had other plans.

I began to write the Rx for L.I.F.E., a daily devotional for Living In Faith Everyday, during my Christmas vacation December 2016, in my hometown of Vancouver, Washington. As I continued to write throughout 2017 and into 2018, I experienced a deeper connection with Yahweh and the Scriptures. My mind was awakened and my eyes opened; I became refreshed and full of a different energy. I begin to accomplish more than I could have imagined in a short time. I felt my soul being refined by the Holy Spirit's fire, and I became impregnated with the realization of why this was something that needed to be birthed.

My willingness and commitment to write this book is in and of itself evidence of the continuous life-changing experience that I have with God. I have not attended seminary, nor have I attended a Christian college, but I believe it is due to my long-term study of the word and the power of my testimony that qualified me to write this book. Namely, God has used testimonies and education to save my life.

I was born with a passion to learn, and over the past eighteen years, I have read the Bible entirely multiple times and certain books like Proverbs and Psalms more times than I could count. The Scriptures are prescriptions for life — basic instructions that help us become and live better. They are in essence spiritual medicine that we have to take daily in order to harness the powerful healing effect. I am excited to share with you what I have learned, what treated many of my symptoms, and what continues to help me.

No doubt, the entire Bible brings health to us, but this devotional connects you with the healing power of the books of Proverbs and Psalms through the 365 daily entries written. I

Introduction

believe each entry is God-inspired, as I would only write after praying and asking God to open my eyes and mind and teach me what I needed to learn. I am thrilled to share with you the messages the Spirit downloaded into my mind and heart. I pray you find encouragement, health, insights, joy, love, peace, refinement, and all the more that God has for you. It takes discipline to live in and walk in faith, and it demands intention and action on our part. This book will assist you with that! The purpose of this devotional is to encourage your relationship and deepen your intimate time with God. We live in faith every day by reading, praying, believing, trusting in His promises, and doing what His word says.

For the past eighteen years that I have been a Christian, this has been my charge. I was briefly introduced to church at a young age but was by no means raised in a Christian home. Growing up, I never knew God. I didn't know if I even believed in God, and I certainly did not think God believed in me. As an adult, I look back and see how much my family and I would have benefitted from truly knowing Him. Like many hardworking American families, we have our strengths, but the cords of societal and socioeconomic injustice coupled with behavioral health issues, abuse, and dysfunction became generational chains that held us tightly entangled. Being born into it, my lot was cast at birth.

My existence is the result of teenage pregnancy. My mother was a single parent and my father died by gunshot when I was six years old. I have no memories of him. My mom sacrificed her late teens, twenties, and thirties to raise me. Oftentimes she would work two jobs to make ends meet. If you have been or know someone in this situation, then you are aware of the high levels of stress, tension, anger, and depression that come with it. Without proper education, psychosocial resources, and God, we were truly helpless. I have seen a lot and experienced a lot of good and bad. My first thoughts of suicide were around my elementary and middle school years. Depression and anxiety would soon come for me in my teens and followed me into adulthood. I ran away from home when I was sixteen years old and later moved to California when I was eighteen years old.

For the next ten years I would go on an adventure of great academic and career highs and self-destructive lows marked by depression, anxiety, and suicidal ideation. I came to know God in my early twenties thanks to a long

Introduction

lost angel of a friend who invited me to church. After a few visits to Antioch Missionary Baptist Church in Oakland, California, I accepted Jesus as my savior and was baptized in August 2000. Although I had come to believe in God, my walk with Jehovah Jireh went up and down. During all of my twenties and early thirties, I seemed to repeat the same mistakes, and I suffered greatly for making poor choices. Facing the serious consequences of being a fool in my own folly was forced self-reflection that slowly led me to know God and get my life in order.

I realized Yahweh had always been there, even when I didn't believe. But once I decided to take time to honestly seek and learn about God, His word, the church, and worship, Yahweh showed up and showed out in my life in ways I could not have imagined. I began to notice changes in my thought life that translated into living differently. As I began to transform, I knew in my heart that I couldn't keep the best Rx for life a secret. I had to share with others the truth: that God could help them change their life, overcome and manage all the yucky stuff that they did and that had happened to them.

I understand emotional, physical, and spiritual pain all too well, but I also know it can be harnessed for our good. How do I know that? I live it! One day my life changed and I experienced an undeniable shift in my mind, and my eyes were illuminated. I now know what and who keeps me alive. Allow me to share with you the spiritual medicine that I have used, the regimen I have personally put into practice and have seen work in my life. God has a purpose for each one of us.

Hands down, I have grown so much mentally, physically, and spiritually from reading, studying, and meditating on the Proverbs and Psalms. Each time I read them, I learn something new or relearn and solidify something I knew before. When you are lost as I was and have a lot of painful and ugly thoughts, your mind needs a cleansing, just the same as when your body is dirty. I experienced a true and much-needed washing of my brain with the profound wisdom, knowledge, and raw emotion expressed in the teachings. The Proverbs and Psalms have helped me to learn how to deal with the everyday ups and downs of life. They teach us how to interact with and care for self, others, community, God, and the government and how to worship. In addition, Psalms are songs that teach us how to worship and have a

Introduction

conversation with God. The playlist is intense and gives full vent to our anger, sorrows, fears, frustrations, joys, and successes. These books teach us how to live in faith every day. They are our prescriptions for L.I.F.E.

A GUIDE TO USING THIS DEVOTIONAL

This devotional contains 365 entries, one written specifically for each day of the year. I believe each entry is what Jah wanted to communicate through me, to me, and to all who will read this book. Regardless of one's belief in Yeshua or not, the word of God remains true. The one who chooses to seek God out and to journey with Him will indeed find Him. In order to experience the fullness of God, our relationship with Him demands time and attention. He needs this time to sift us, teach us, heal us, and transform us. The Proverbs and Psalms both direct us in the areas of interpersonal relationships, career, business, spiritual diets, physical diets, self-care, mental and behavioral health, parenting, law, and more.

This book was written with the intent to help guide your study and prayer time. The year has been left off intentionally to allow the book a timeless legacy. You will need a Bible when using this devotional, and you will be reading the books Proverbs and Psalms. This devotional was written referencing verses from the New International Version, NIV, of The Holy Bible. Other versions may be used, but please note that the verses may read slightly different.

There are 31 Proverbs and 150 Psalms. Begin studying the Proverbs by reading one Proverb each day. This is what I did to learn. It is easy to follow because there are more or less thirty days in each month so that every month we are able to read the entire book of Proverbs. By the time you finish the year, you will have read through all the Proverbs twelve times! Remember, the word "pro" means for, supporting, and movement forward, and "verbs" almost always involve action.

I have also included additional inspiration from the Psalms handpicked to complement the Proverb selected for the day. Although each devotional highlights one Proverb each day and a recommended reading from Psalms, the challenge is for you to read the entire Proverb that corresponds to that day of the month. Over the year you will grow wiser, stronger, and more courageous. You will indeed experience

Introduction

---

a transformation. There is no way you will stay the same.

Example: If today is January 8, 2019, you would be reading and meditating on a verse from Proverb 8 and a corresponding message.

You will also notice the use of different names of God throughout. These are meant to give you more of an intimate experience with God, and being able to call Him by name is an important part of that closeness. Please reference the glossary at the end of the book for meanings of different names of God and words.

Whether you have been a Christian for many years or a short while, you will gain from studying the Proverbs and Psalms and using this book. And if you are not a Christian, meaning you have not accepted Christ as your savior, you can still benefit. I would be remiss to not extend to you the opportunity to accept God in your life and Jesus Christ as your savior. No one is perfect. We have all made mistakes and will make them until we die. Yet Jesus came to die for our sins in order to restore our relationship with God. If we believe that He is who He says He is and confess with our lips that we are sinners and declare that Jesus died for us, we are saved. I invite you to do that now if you have never asked God to live in your heart.

If you would like to make that decision now and ask God into your life, just say the following:

Dear God,

I know that I have sinned and have been living in my own strength. I know that Jesus Christ died for my sins. I thank you for your gift of salvation, and I want to accept it today. I invite you in my heart and mind and surrender my life to you. In the name of Jesus, Amen!

If you prayed that prayer, God bless you! Plug in to a community of like-minded believers and get ready for the journey of a lifetime.

Please know that even though we may not know each other personally, I am standing with you in prayer. I encourage you to really dive in to your devotion time and get the healing you need to continue to live in faith every day, to live L.I.F.E. I believe the journey of life is about learning and getting better, little by little, every day. I made up a mantra a few years ago for myself, and it has helped me to focus on one day at a time. "Today be better than you were

Introduction

yesterday and tomorrow better than you are today." I quote it on every page so you can see it as you take your daily devotional dose of inspiration with God.

I pray that God fills your spirit with more peace, love, joy, gentleness, kindness, and self-control. My hope is that those who don't know God will come to know Him, and for those who do know Him, that their relationship with Him will be fully realized. I pray God meets you right where you are and shows up in such a real way that it cannot be denied that it is you, God. Amen!

I would love to hear from you. Please share your feedback, and if this book changes your life in the slightest bit, tell somebody. Pass it along! I thank you for your time and purchase and I wish you all the best in your life journey. Shalom!

Love,
Malieka

JANUARY

My son, pay attention to my wisdom,
listen well to my words of insight.
                              Proverb 5:1

January 1

Proverb 1:2
Wisdom

My friend, we must desire and commit to living wise and disciplined lives. These intentional acts are pleasing to Yahweh and beneficial to us. Wisdom won't let us down! How many times have you said or heard the words exclaimed, "If only I had known." The awareness in that statement acknowledges that wisdom has a place in our lives.

Trust and believe that only with God can we know and understand anything. Let us make a commitment to search for knowledge and do what is right. Jehovah will then be pleased to give us words of insight. Shalom!

Additional Inspiration: Psalm 119:66

January 2

Proverb 2:2-3
Applying

Today we are called to action by turning our ear, applying our heart, and calling out. As we would turn our head toward a speaker to hear them and listen more intently, Yah wants us to respond this way to Him. We can hear our Creator speak to us through the wisdom of wise counsel while reading the Scriptures or by hearing directly from the Counselor. We must not only listen with our ears but also with our hearts, where our inner core resides. Insight: He even tells us to "cry aloud." I dare you to try it. Shalom!

Additional Inspiration: Psalm 119:73

Rx: Today be better than you were yesterday and tomorrow better than you are today. ~Dr. J

January 3

Proverb 3:3
Faithfulness

The imagery of this Proverb paints a picture of Yahweh asking us to become intimately engaged with love and faithfulness. Much like clothes, jewelry, and food, God wants love and faithfulness on us, bound to our neck, and within us on our heart. Imagine it being that simple to activate love and faithfulness by wearing them on a necklace or downloading them to our "iHeart tablet." This is not quite our fortune; however, we do possess the power to be cognizant of love and faithfulness and to choose them daily. Shalom!

Additional Inspiration: Psalm 119:10–11

Rx: Today be better than you were yesterday and tomorrow better than you are today. ~Dr. J

January 4

Proverb 4:1
Attention

Eyes open + Ears open + Mind alert = Insight. This verse tells us to listen and pay attention. Both actions require a certain level of awareness at all times. Information comes at us from numerous sources and at varying speeds. It is hard to keep up and to truly fact check everything. Even our parents, friends, and colleagues can give us faulty advice or set poor examples.

We can learn from listening and paying attention both what to do and what not to do in various situations. In addition, Yahweh promises that we will gain understanding when we align with Him. As a soldier stands attention, assume your position and be blessed. Shalom!

Additional Inspiration: Psalm 25:8

Rx: Today be better than you were yesterday and tomorrow better than you are today. ~Dr. J

January 5

Proverb 5:1
Insight

Wake up and pay attention! Awake o' sleeper and listen to God calling you. We have been given the command to take action, to listen, and to attend. How much would you pay to gain insight into your life decisions? We deliberate for days, weeks, months, and sometimes years about this decision and that option. We ask which way to go or where to remain.

We must recognize that the answers and in-depth knowledge we are looking for are embedded in the Lord. When we read His word and pray and listen for Him, He will indeed speak to our spirits. Keep pressing forward in the Holy Spirit. Shalom!

Additional Inspiration: Psalm 25:5

January 6

Proverb 6:2–3
Humble

It's never too late to say "I'm sorry" to someone you may have offended by something you said. We must realize what a destructive tool the mouth can be. God gives us so much instruction in the Scriptures about watching our mouth and controlling our tongue. It is a small part of the body that can either build another up or verbally murder them. If we are going to err, let us err on the side of saying too little, rather than too much.

Make it an active part of your life to monitor your speech. Don't be deceived by the laws of man; we don't have freedom of speech in the spiritual world. What comes out of your mouth dictates how you experience your life, marriage, job, and health. Let's think more before we speak. Change of heart leads to change of mind, and change of speech. Shalom!

Additional Inspiration: Psalm 141:3

Rx: Today be better than you were yesterday and tomorrow better than you are today. ~Dr. J

January 7

Proverb 7:1
Store

This is a call to action! We are in the process of becoming storekeepers of the word of God. Over and over throughout the Scriptures, especially Proverbs, we see the call to action to produce fruit. As created humans, we essentially work for God, and our job is to produce. We have a daily choice to choose actions that will lead to good fruit or bad fruit.

Therefore, our lives and all that we are involved in is proof of our production. When we keep and store the Word of God in us, it will be evident by the fruit we bear. Pray, read, meditate, and discuss with others. This will increase your desire to grow in your faith. Amen!

Additional Inspiration: Psalm 119:33–34

Rx: Today be better than you were yesterday and tomorrow better than you are today. ~Dr. J

January 8

Proverb 8:4–5
Simple

Dear friends, our Creator developed a healthy and holistic lifestyle for us. He teaches us His methods through reading Scripture, praying, and meditating. As you read this Proverb, take note that Yahweh does not promise wisdom only to Christians or Jews. It clearly says that wisdom poses herself for all to hear and see. She, wisdom, raises her voice to all mankind. This covers every continent without question.

We human beings are faced with the ultimate mystery of choice. We have freedom whether we like it or not, and in turn the choices we make have automatic consequences, good and/or bad. The blessing is that we can enlist help in this area by using prudence and seeking understanding. All we have to do is ask, listen, and act. Shalom!

Additional Inspiration: Psalm 1:2

Rx: Today be better than you were yesterday and tomorrow better than you are today. ~Dr. J

January 9

Proverb 9:1–2
Wisdom

Preparation is the key to success. When we decide upon a goal, it is first believing that we can achieve it and then preparing for the journey to accomplish it. Wisdom tells us that we must use good judgment if we want to have productive, healthy, successful lives. "Build your house first" means secure your home on a firm foundation.

Seven pillars represent perfection and stability. Once your shelter is secure, get your nourishment squared away. After that, set your table in preparation. Stay ready and be alert. Success is at your fingertips. Shalom!

Additional Inspiration: Psalm 115:12–13

Rx: Today be better than you were yesterday and tomorrow better than you are today. ~Dr. J

January 10

Proverb 10:4
Diligent

Yes, Lord, we want to be blessed. We happily accept your double portion of diligence. Jehovah worked six days and rested one. He recommended us to do the same—not the reverse, work only one day and rest six. The Word says if a man will not work, he shall not eat.

While we must always be sensitive to those who physically or mentally cannot work, we must also expect those who are able-bodied to contribute to society. There is really no excuse to miss this blessing. The wealth that comes from being diligent may be in the form of finances, career, relationships, or health. Get ready to be blessed. Shalom!

Additional Inspiration: Psalm 84:11–12

Rx: Today be better than you were yesterday and tomorrow better than you are today. ~Dr. J

January 11

Proverb 11:1
Accurate

We are made in the image of our Creator having the same emotions, feelings, and intelligence. Therefore, it should come as no surprise that we can be bothered by that which offends our Father. This Proverb makes it clear that God is detailed, honest, fair, and accurate. This is evident by the fantastically detailed crafted creation in which we exist.

Injustice, dishonest gain, and inaccurate life and business transactions not only upset God, but it makes many of us angry too. This is a healthy spiritual response that is in the image of our maker. This should force us to give thought to our ways and to be aware of how honest, fair, and accurate we are in our daily business dealings and personal relationships. Meditate on this today. Shalom!

Additional Inspiration: Psalm 98:7–9

January 12

Proverb 12:1
Stupid

Many of us were raised to not call ourselves or anyone else the word "stupid." Well, funny that God looks at us as such when we refuse correction. We are creatures of habit, whether the habit is good or bad. We will simply remain in that fashion until we are either forced to change or desire to.

Yahweh teaches us throughout this Proverb that discipline and being open to change are two keys for success in life. We gain knowledge when we accept correction. In that exchange, we grow wiser and become more of who we are supposed to be. Good thing we serve a merciful and patient God who gives us new days to begin new ways. Shalom!

Additional Inspiration: Psalm 119:56

Rx: Today be better than you were yesterday and tomorrow better than you are today. ~Dr. J

January 13

Proverb 13:2
Faithful

The saying "You will eat your words" really applies here. Our speech has power and must be used appropriately. We have the ability to speak good or bad into our life and others' lives. We can easily become aligned with the mantras we hear most often, whether internally or externally. We must be mindful of this as we are in the process of life transformation.

Be patient with yourself, but remember to speak life into yourself and others. Lift others up with encouraging and inspiring words, thoughts, and actions. As we sow good seed into ourselves and others, we reap the blessings that Yahweh harvests for us. Shalom!

Additional Inspiration: Psalm 16:2

January 14

Proverb 14:1
Wise

When we consider the ways that God provides for us, we ought to value our blessings more. It's hard to keep this idea constantly at the forefront of our minds, but it's important. When we walk with God in wisdom and show respect to ourselves, other people, and the gifts He has given us, it allows God to bless us more abundantly. He sees that we trust Him, and we are appreciative.

When we disrespect ourselves, others, and the gifts He has given us, we slowly begin to lose everything—our mind, relationships, and treasures. When we head down that path, we feel increased depression, stress, and anxiety, and often blame God. This verse cries woe to us. Pray and make wise choices daily so you can live life abundantly. Shalom!

Additional Inspiration: Psalm 18:28–29

Rx: Today be better than you were yesterday and tomorrow better than you are today. ~Dr. J

January 15

Proverb 15:1
Gentle

We know that our words have power. Genesis Chapter 1 tells us that God spoke the world and universe into existence. There is soul power in the tongue. The Scriptures indicate that from the heart of a man/woman so he/she speaks. Friends, if we truly want to live a Christian life, if we truly want to follow Yeshua, then we must align ourselves with this Proverb. This way of thinking is clutch. We must be diligent seekers of peace and sensor our speech. We are learning and growing together. Keep this in prayer. Shalom!

Additional Inspiration: Psalm 145:8

January 16

Proverb 16:1
Reply

The architect may have a blueprint but still requires the city planner to approve the build. Even with a well-written business plan, it is still the "yes" reply from the lender or investor that allows the project to be realized. In the same way, we have plans, big plans, little plans, and no plans. We can spend our time over-planning, under-planning, or not planning at all. Amen to God if you have ever had a situation that "just worked itself out." Ultimately, God has the final word!

God is by no means telling us to not plan. Quite the opposite, He wants us to plan but to be sensitive to His reply and His direction for our lives, whether His reply is wait, no, or yes. Always remember that He knows best. Consult with Him for everything in order to align your life with His will for you. Shalom!

Additional Inspiration: Psalm 57:2

Rx: Today be better than you were yesterday and tomorrow better than you are today. ~Dr. J

January 17

Proverb 17:1
Strife

My mother was a teenage single parent. She tried to go on welfare for a short time, but according to her, she did not like the government cheese. Instead she had to work two jobs to make ends meet. We ate out a lot as a consequence. It was nothing too fancy, but to a kid, I was living the life with continual happy meals, Red Robin, and Olive Garden. Growing up I looked forward to my grandmother's deliciously prepared holiday meals. However, our family dysfunction would produce strife and those delicious meals would quickly be disrupted with arguments.

As I read this Proverb, I wondered what would have been if we had accepted the dry crust with that government cheese. If you have experienced anything similar or know someone who is, remember peace and love is the key to living life in harmony with others on this earth. Let's think and let's pray. Shalom!

Additional Inspiration: Psalm 29:11

Rx: Today be better than you were yesterday and tomorrow better than you are today. ~Dr. J

January 18

Proverb 18:2
Understanding

"Oh, yeah, you talk too much! Homeboy, you never shut up!" This line from 1990s female rap group Salt-N-Pepa comes to mind when reading this passage. Communication is vital to our existence, and there is definitely an art to dialoguing with others. A certain level of social etiquette is usually observed within cultures. Listening is one such rule. We learn when we listen.

A person who talks ad nauseam and never takes time to listen possesses arrogance and self-centeredness. We should always carry healthy self-esteem, but we should also stay other-centered. This helps us to foster healthy relationships. Because it is not always easy to do, we must continuously ask Yahweh to humble our hearts and not be the fool. Selah!

Additional Inspiration: Psalm 12:3–4

Rx: Today be better than you were yesterday and tomorrow better than you are today. ~Dr. J

January 19

Proverb 19:2
Zeal

Have you ever shared news or an idea with someone and they basically told you, "Hold up. Don't get too excited." Of course you felt like they were trying to kill your vibe. Oftentimes God does the same thing, but He does it out of love and protection of our vibe. We can get easily excited about people, places, and things and have little to no information about them. We can be so excited about getting somewhere and literally miss our exit!

When you feel hasty or overzealous, take heed to this Proverb. Present every petition to the Lord so He can be the lamp unto your feet. God promises to keep us from the perils and traps that so easily ensnare. Amen!

Additional Inspiration: Psalm 143:7

January 20

Proverb 20:1
Mocker

Many of us know someone affected by alcoholism. Many of us also know first-hand the effects of drinking too much. Although God gave us beer, wine, and spirits to enjoy, we must remember that they are mind-altering substances that require full self-control when we use them. As this Proverb indicates, it is simply unwise to lose your life to drinking too much.

This further applies to any addictive behavior that leads to the loss of life. If we want to be blessed, we need to think wise and practice making wise decisions. No one should ever feel ashamed for admitting to needing and getting help. Those are action steps of a warrior. Be brave and be healed. Selah!

Additional Inspiration: Psalm 143:1–2

Rx: Today be better than you were yesterday and tomorrow better than you are today. ~Dr. J

January 21

Proverb 21:2
Weighs

No one knows the absolute truth of another's heart except that person and God. Even if we share what is on our heart, we can always choose to keep something to ourselves. Oftentimes we get misled into thinking we are not bad people because we don't commit any grandiose law-breaking sins. You may have told yourself once or twice, "I'm a good person," and while that may be your truth, sometimes we do good things for selfish reasons. God ultimately knows our heart and understands our motives. We may fool one another, but we cannot and do not fool our Creator. Be wise, be blessed, and stay humble. Shalom!

Additional Inspiration: Psalm 90:8

January 22

Proverb 22:2
Common

Every human being is important in the eyes of God. Yahweh is indeed concerned about our socioeconomic status. This is why He gives us commands to share out of abundance with those who don't have. This is also why He warns the rich to not oppress and take advantage of those in need. Jehovah cares because He loves us! Let's stay aware of how we treat one another and make an effort to remember to love others as He loves us. Shalom!

Additional Inspiration: Psalm 8:4–5

Rx: Today be better than you were yesterday and tomorrow better than you are today. ~Dr. J

January 23

Proverb 23:4
Restraint

One piece of advice a college professor gave me was to "Study what you love and the money will come." If we do what we are designed to do, we won't have to wear ourselves out with odd jobs to make ends meet or get rich. Notice the Proverb says, "Don't wear yourself out to get rich." It doesn't say that there's anything wrong with wealth. Money can do a great deal of good for everyone.

Yahweh wants us to have active scales, always weigh pros and cons, and evaluate ourselves and the situation. We often make poor decisions when we let our love of money guide our lives rather than the love of fulfilling our purpose. Use wisdom and show restraint. Shalom!

Additional Inspiration: Psalm 49:12

January 24

Proverb 24:3-4
Knowledge

This Proverb speaks to who and what we rely on to provide us a firm foundation and how we can maximize bearing good fruit. Yahweh explains that we gain our covering, our shelter, from Him by being wise enough to ask Him. When we accept the Lord as our savior, we begin the process of building our new house with God. We continue journeying with Him through prayer, study, meditation, attending church, memorizing scripture, joining small groups, and getting involved in ministry.

All these actions help us gain the understanding we need and further establishes our home and new position in Christ. When we repeat the above, we grow ever more in knowledge and relationship with God, and He uses this as a way to continuously fill us with His Holy Spirit. This in turn allows our unique gifts, our rare and beautiful treasures, to be manifested. Be blessed. Shalom!

Additional Inspiration: Psalm 119:4

Rx: Today be better than you were yesterday and tomorrow better than you are today. ~Dr. J

January 25

Proverb 25:4
Dross

When we consider the purification process for our objects of silver and gold, we gain some perspective from the wisdom of our glorious and Holy God. If Yahweh cares enough to give us a process by which we can make inanimate objects shine, then it is not a stretch to believe that He has a process by which He is refining us to enable Himself to shine through us. When we let Him do the work, we are His craftsmanship and He is glorified. Hallelujah for dross removal. No more yucky stuff. Shalom!

Additional Inspiration: Psalm 31:16

January 26

Proverb 26:1
Honor

Things that make you go *hmm*. Snow in the summer and rain during a harvest are out of place with the season. When these events occur, we usually think, "This isn't right." Oddly enough, Yahweh compares this to a fool having honor, an anomaly. Many of us may feel this way about leaders we see in our workplaces or portrayed through the media lens. We wonder, "How did they get that position?"

While it may be easy for us to see this in others, it can be hard to recognize it in ourselves. Ouch! It's time for your fool maintenance check. Is there something you need to let go of before you can be honored? Just do it; drop it, leave it, and let it go. Selah!

Additional Inspiration: Psalm 53:1

Rx: Today be better than you were yesterday and tomorrow better than you are today. ~Dr. J

January 27

Proverb 27:1
Boast

With so many social media platforms and ways to communicate, we are constantly barraged with "what's next." We know each other's daily play-by-play! Most sports teams keep their playbook top secret, and only those who need to know are privy to this information. This is not to suggest that we live a life of complete secrecy. Rather a call to give thought to our motivation for sharing what we are doing, eating, seeing, etc. The word says if we think more of ourselves than we are, we so deceive ourselves. If we boast, let us boast in Christ and of His mercy, grace and love. Amen!

Additional Inspiration: Psalm 109:26–27

January 28

Proverb 28:2
Rebellious

This Proverb truly speaks to the times we are in. When a country has many rulers and is rebellious, there are currents of chaos, confusion, and uncertainty that run throughout the community nervous system. Everyone can sense that something just doesn't feel right. Although we may feel extremely helpless in these times, Yah wants us to remember Him and His word. We can carry peace within us and within our circles of influence by exercising understanding and knowledge. We can keep order in the midst of the storm. Don't be afraid to walk on the water. Shalom!

Additional Inspiration: Psalm 82:8

January 29

Proverb 29:1
Stiff-Necked

Dear friend, as we journey through this experience, we must constantly take inventory of who we are and what we stand for. If we desire to live the right life, we must act in accordance so that we are actually living out what we envision or imagine. Some of us are very stubborn or hardheaded. Others of us have false expectations of people and situations. In the interim, we find ourselves caught up in a web of habits, lifestyles, conversations, actions, behaviors, and thoughts that don't allow us to thrive.

When we become anesthetized to the warning signs and persist in our folly, we encounter the consequences of poor choices. Thankfully we have a Father in Heaven who, just in growing us up, is also tender to love us through a stiff neck. Shalom!

Additional Inspiration: Psalm 32:5–6

Rx: Today be better than you were yesterday and tomorrow better than you are today. ~Dr. J

January 30

Proverb 30:2
Wisdom

Dear Friends, coming to this reality can be one of the most freeing moments of our lives. With all the amazing advances people groups of all societies have made, we still don't know everything. Researchers and scientists are still searching an unsearchable universe and getting more and more blown away by what is discovered. We can't Google everything we want to know, but it sure comes in handy.

As amazingly created as we are, we must get comfortable with the fact that we are limited in our thinking, what information we know, and our physical abilities. Humble yourself and relax in that truth. Don't feel like you need to know and do it all. Pray for God to give you wisdom and understanding, and it will go well with you. Shalom!

Additional Inspiration: Psalm 111:10

Rx: Today be better than you were yesterday and tomorrow better than you are today. ~Dr. J

January 31

Proverb 31:8
Destitute

We are given the charge to care for the needy and the voiceless. This shouldn't be an option for us, but too often it is. It is hard to believe that in the twenty-first century, with all the inventions and advances in human knowledge across all fields and sectors, we still have people facing varying degrees of poverty. In America the poverty line is considered rich in comparison to other countries. These realities are absolutely mind-boggling!

Some of us humans use these disparities as an excuse to question God. We shake our fist at the Creator and deny Him completely. Sadly this is the wrong approach. We are frustrated with the wrong person. God doesn't cause all of our socioeconomic disparities. We the people play a big role in creating division. Let's think and act. This is what we are called to. When we do unto the least of these, we do it unto Yah and we bring Him pleasure. Shalom!

Additional Inspiration: Psalm 103:6

FEBRUARY

Keep my commands and you will live; guard my teachings as the apple of your eye.

Proverb 7:2

February 1

Proverb 1:3
Prudent

Dear friend, if we want better lives, we must learn to trust the word of Yah. The Holy Bible, also known as "Basic Instructions Before Leaving Earth," promotes learning and understanding through direct and indirect examples, teachings, and metaphors. While we don't need to go to seminary to gain this wisdom, it would behoove us to put a similar effort and structure into our learning in order that we gain the wisdom, knowledge, and understanding that is available to us. A professional doesn't gain their title from a lack of knowledge. Rather, it's the time spent reading and working with the literature that allows one to profess himself or herself as a professional.

Our Creator wants us to have a deeper understanding of Him and a profound spiritual walk with Him. Our spirit affects our entire being, and when we neglect our spirit, we experience consequences in our mind and physical realms. It's not a coincidence you're reading this today. Continue in your curiosity to learn more, and you will be enlightened. Study the word, be bold, and profess what you know. These teachings will help us do what is right, just, and fair. Amen!

Additional Inspiration: Psalm 119:59–60

February 2

Proverb 2:4–5
Search

Did you ever play hide-and-seek as a child? For some reason it felt good to be found, and it was fun to seek. Let's face it: anything worth having is worth searching out, learning, and working for. As such, we must work at those things we wish to perfect. We know that learning and application don't happen by osmosis. We must be active to physically see fruit in our lives.

We attain a fruitful life by seeking first the things of God's kingdom and then aligning our life mission with our Creator. Yahweh makes it clear that we must be active participants in our quest to find Him. A reverent fear is the beginning of understanding. Find encouragement as you read, pray, write, and have fellowship with like-minded people. Jehovah wants to reveal Himself to us, so let the search begin! Amen!

Additional Inspiration: Psalm 2:4–5

February 3

Proverb 3:4
Favor

We have all heard the statement, "I don't care what people think of me or what they say about me." While it is scripture to not put our trust in man alone, it is also a promise of God that we will gain favor with people. If we are honest, we can admit that we enjoy the feeling of being liked. If you have ever experienced not being liked, loved, favored, or valued, you know it's a cruddy feeling. Most of us want our name to be well-thought of and our reputation to be respected. Yahweh teaches us to let the action of love and faithfulness rule in our lives so that we will win favor and a good name not only with Him, but with our peers. Now that's what we call a "twofer." Amen!

Additional Inspiration: Psalm 112:1

Rx: Today be better than you were yesterday and tomorrow better than you are today. ~Dr. J

February 4

Proverb 4:2
Forsake

Realize that we don't always receive full understanding of what we are learning, but we do know that with God, the learning we receive has purpose and meaning. Our Father isn't giving us the "because I said so" response. In some ways we may not be ready for all that He knows about a given person or situation, but we can rest assured that He has our back. Jehovah will never turn His back on us. We are always safe and sound with Him. Amen!

Additional Inspiration: Psalm 119:27

February 5

Proverb 5:2
Discretion

Yahweh is interested in right living. He wants us to experience the best that He has for us while we are on earth. This is why it is written, "Our Father in heaven hallowed be thy name, your kingdom come, your will be done on earth as it is in heaven." God doesn't want to hide Himself from us or deprive us of a good life. Not at all! He actually wants us to have a long, abundant life.

We accomplish this by practicing His way of living. When we are full of His love and wisdom, our lips will preserve knowledge and we maintain discretion. God is working everything together for the good of those who love Him. Hallelujah!

Additional Inspiration: Psalm 39:1

Rx: Today be better than you were yesterday and tomorrow better than you are today. ~Dr. J

February 6

Proverb 6:6–8
Wise

Remember the good ole days when we were kids and we had someone to hold us accountable? Of course, as kids we didn't see it that way; we just had nagging parents. As adults we have so much to tend to, yet some of us find it hard to get motivated enough to start and complete many tasks, goals, and dreams. The ant, something so small you may not even realize that you kill one, is considered wise and proactive in the eyes of God.

The ants don't wait for team encouragement to begin and finish their work. The ant has a strong work ethic and takes care of business. We need to get comfortable with holding three positions of power: coach, player, and fan. Let Yahweh be the referee. He will tell you when to take your time out. Stay grinding, keep hustling, be fruitful, and multiply. Amen!

Additional Inspiration: Psalm 19:7

Rx: Today be better than you were yesterday and tomorrow better than you are today. ~Dr. J

February 7

Proverb 7:2
Keep

More action required! Yahweh is asking us once again to put into use what He has given us—His very word. His "Basic Instructions Before Leaving Earth," is our Bible. God breathed the scriptures that have been handed down for thousands of years, and He wants us to commit them to our heart, mind, and spirit. The more you pray, read, and meditate, the more life you will have. What are you esteeming as the apple of your eye? Remember to reserve that space for God Most High. Shalom!

Additional Inspiration: Psalm 119:17–18

February 8

Proverb 8:6-7
Listen

Trust in God, He will never lead us astray. It is hard for many of us to hear God speak, so we think He doesn't converse with us. This logic is exactly what the enemy uses to bait us and how he wants us to think about our Father. But, we should not be so easily deceived. Our God would not instruct us to listen if He didn't desire to communicate with us. We easily take time to listen to worldly advice from our friends, family, talk-show hosts, radio personalities, bloggers, and even magazine advice columnists. None of these sources can guarantee us that they have worthy things to say or the right advice.

Practice setting aside time to pray and listen. Listen for God to prompt your spirit through the help of the Holy Spirit. Remember, God often speaks quietly to us and with a still, small voice. This lifestyle takes time and effort on our part, but we will be happily rewarded with a firm path and sweet sleep. Amen!

Additional Inspiration: Psalm 48:14

Rx: Today be better than you were yesterday and tomorrow better than you are today. ~Dr. J

February 9

Proverb 9:4 and 9:16
Judgment

This verse is repeated twice in Proverb 9, and with good reason. Yahweh really wants us to learn this principle. The world will call out to you and tempt you in many different ways, appealing to all your senses. In some ways, media and advertising exploit the psychology of humans to get us to buy their products. If it didn't work, companies wouldn't spend billions of dollars annually in the form of radio, print, digital, and television ads. I'm not saying that we should not advertise; this is a part of business. Yet it is to say, be on guard at all times. We are told in the book of James that the enemy, Satan, prowls and lurks around looking for those to devour. Seek God on everything and make decisions with Godly counsel. Selah!

Additional Inspiration: Psalm 19:8

February 10

Proverb 10:8
Chattering

Dear friends, we look to find an answer for everything. We engage in self-talk, dialogue with friends, and endless Internet searches in hopes to get the clue we need to make sense of our situation. We get lost in a sea of self-rationalized excuses and friends concurring with us so we feel better. This can lead to pseudo-justification, and at the end of the cycle, we are right back where we started, lost. God wants more for us.

We must daily prepare our hearts and minds to be in communion with the Creator. He puts the right people and circumstances in our path at just the right time. We must be open to His instructions and be ready to act. So, chatter away excuses and go get the blessings waiting for you. Amen!

Additional Inspiration: Psalm 10:4–7

Rx: Today be better than you were yesterday and tomorrow better than you are today. ~Dr. J

February 11

Proverb 11:3
Duplicity

When we lead a life of integrity, it means we are in a state of being complete and have the quality of being honest and fair. A person of integrity follows and adheres to a code of morals and operates on sound principles. When we walk in a state of duplicity, we are being, in layman's terms, fake, two-faced, and double-minded. This type of person plays games as seen carried out in the mini dramas of life.

God actually says stay on guard around people like this because their crafty, cunning behavior can appear harmless, but like Satan in the Garden of Eden, they are clever and wait to corrupt your spirit. God says they will eat the fruit of their deceptive ways as a result of their behavior. Walk upright and let the Lord bless you. Selah!

Additional Inspiration: Psalm 96:13

February 12

Proverb 12:2
Condemns

At first pass when you read this Proverb and consider our present world, it may seem that this Proverb is untrue. So much craftiness, deception, greed, waste, fraud, and the like is occurring on our watch. It turns many of us off and can often make people question their faith. Evil works may seem to be rewarded on earth, and that is where the deceiver attempts to confuse us and take hold of our thoughts. However, God is still watching!

Hallelujah, He sees our good works and we will be rewarded. We are encouraged to not tire of doing good. According to Adonai, prosperity and life are waiting on the other side. Stay upright in your dealings, and God will bless you abundantly. Watch, play, and see. Amen!

Additional Inspiration: Psalm 140:6–8

Rx: Today be better than you were yesterday and tomorrow better than you are today. ~Dr. J

February 13

Proverb 13:3
Rashly

Throughout Scripture, God makes it clear that our mouths can ruin us. It is very easy for us to speak quickly without giving thought to the consequences of our words. Listen and observe when people talk too much or too loose. If you find yourself doing either or both, ask God to help you strengthen in this area. He wants the best for us and will always answer our prayers to improve self-control. Don't feel that you have to join in the gab. It's better to be silent than to say something that hurts another and we later regret. Amen!

Additional Inspiration: Psalm 17:3

February 14

Proverb 14:8
Deception

Dear friends, in order to live the good life we so desire, we must give thought to our ways. Our ways include what we think, say, and do. Our ways are a reflection of our heart condition. When we take the posture that we can say what we want, think what we please, and do as we wish, we are foolish and so deceive ourselves.

Apostle Paul explains that when he was a child, he thought and acted childlike. But as an adult, with the knowledge of Jesus Christ, he had to mature in his ways. We must put childish mannerisms behind us and be the mature spiritual beings that we were created to be. Pray and keep seeking wisdom. Shalom!

Additional Inspiration: Psalm 119:59–60

February 15

Proverb 15:3
Wicked

El Shaddai Adonai is an omnipotent, omnipresent, omniscient God! It is so easy to forget this because we see good and evil all around us. From the local news to international reports to social media updates, we see chaos and order. Unexpected phone calls from friends and family can be either tragedy or triumph. For some of us, at certain points in our life, we may wonder where is God in all this.

But don't lose heart. He knows and understands. God doesn't love us any less. In fact, He appreciates that we can still discern good from bad. We must remember that Yah still has a plan and we are on His timeline. Be still and know God is God. No one and no thing is hidden from Him. Shalom!

Additional Inspiration: Psalm 33:13–15

February 16

Proverb 16:2
Motives

True enough, the only person to know your heart intention is you, God, and whomever you choose to share your truth with. We must be honest with ourselves about our intentions in what we do and what we say. Humans have the unique ability to mask our true selves from others. This is why we are easily surprised when a friend, family member, or a coworker acts in a way not conducive to what we've known of them. Sometimes we find ourselves experiencing negative consequences of decisions we've made after getting involved in something for the wrong reasons.

It takes spiritual maturity to put yourself under a microscope, but the report can yield lifelong lasting benefits. Let our motives be good, true, and pure in heart. Then Yahweh can be glorified and make changes in our life. Amen!

Additional Inspiration: Psalm 15:1–5

Rx: Today be better than you were yesterday and tomorrow better than you are today. ~Dr. J

February 17

Proverb 17:5
Gloat

This verse is very humbling and should remind us to exercise restraint and empathy. Many of us have either experienced poking fun at others or have been on the receiving end of ridicule. Both are places we should never be. We should remind ourselves of this and teach our children to not bully. We never know the reason for another person's circumstances, and ours can change at any moment. Be thankful and pray for others less fortunate. Yahweh blesses you today and every day. Amen!

Additional Inspiration: Psalm 102:16–17

February 18

Proverb 18:4
Wisdom

We can easily drown ourselves in negative speech and thoughts. When our hearts' condition stems from a fleshly place, these deep waters can easily swallow us up, as well as those around us. We should exercise caution when we speak. Are you speaking life or death into those you come into contact with? The one who speaks from a spirit-filled place and has a heart condition of love censors their language and tone of speech. In essence, their words become life-giving as a bubbling brook. Praise God that we can refresh one another. Shalom!

Additional Inspiration: Psalm 34:1–3

February 19

Proverb 19:3
Folly

Have you ever heard a person blame God for everything wrong in life? Perhaps you are or were that person. To some degree, many of us at some point in time blame God for this or that which is bad in our lives or the world around us. No doubt we experience sudden tragedies that are no fault of our own. But this Proverb is shedding light on the negative consequences of our own poor choices.

Oftentimes when we have to face the horrible consequences of drug addictions, overspending, porn addictions, infidelity, unsafe sex, gambling, stealing, murder, and so on, we want to blame Yahweh. Isn't it interesting that our hearts would rage against a good God rather than rage against Satan, the ruler of evil? Let's strive to make better decisions daily. Amen!

Additional Inspiration: Psalm 142:6–7

February 20

Proverb 20:3
Fool

Jesus said He came so we could have life and have it abundantly. He also came bearing peace unto us. We must remember this always. God wants and God is both love and peace. If you are an argumentative or quarrelsome person, pray that God begins to help you change and harness more self-control in this area. Just remember that every fool is quick to quarrel, and you are no fool! Avoid strife and seek peace, because when we do, we bring honor to Yahweh. Amen!

Additional Inspiration: Psalm 139:23–24

February 21

Proverb 21:3
Just

Is it possible to sacrifice and not do what is right and just? You bet this is why Jesus had to come. He had to fulfill the law and then be the final sacrifice for us. In the Old Testament there were so many sacrifices made to atone for the people's sins, but they continued in their way. Yahweh's final sacrifice by way of Yeshua freed us from the legalistic ritual sacrifice and entered us into grace. God still requires obedience as acceptable sacrifice. Yes, it can be hard, but we can choose to do right—and when we do, we will be blessed even more. Amen!

Additional Inspiration: Psalm 106:3

February 22

Proverb 22:3
Prudent

Sometime we are just plain hardheaded! It doesn't matter how old we get; some of us are not interested in heeding instruction and thus suffer consequences. The error that often takes place is our displaced aggression after we endure the negative outcome. If we don't stop to recognize our foolishness and keep going, we easily shake our fists at God wondering why this or that happened to us. This is called living deceived. No doubt, we will run into trouble in this life however, we can minimize it when Yah has provided ample warning for us to see the danger and take refuge. Amen!

Additional Inspiration: Psalm 86:16–17

February 23

Proverb 23:5
Glance

Have you ever had the experience of wondering where all your money went? Or have you ever been awarded an inheritance or large sum of money only to wonder a short time later how it is all gone? Stock market and housing crashes and bad investments are symbolic of the eagle mounting wings that fly away with the riches.

We know from scripture that God blesses some with riches. This financial blessing is so we can be a blessing to others. Cast but a glance at riches and fix our eyes firmly on Yahweh, and He will secure the rest. We should be mindful to always be good stewards of what we are given. Amen!

Additional Inspiration: Psalm 49: 10–11

February 24

Proverb 24:5
Strength

This is an example of spiritual weight training. Just as our physical muscles need exercise to become stronger, so it is with our spiritual muscles. They must be worked out to get spiritually stronger. At the gym we exercise by engaging our muscle. We seek out the machine or free weights, and we even choose the load we want. When we get serious about our health, we actually make it more difficult for ourselves by increasing the load so we can become more powerful and get the results we want.

Can you see how God uses a similar mechanism for our spiritual growth? He allows for certain trials and tribulations that feel weighty to help shape and grow our character. As He grows us in wisdom, we actually become powerful and increase in strength with more knowledge. This is an eternal promise that only Yahweh can extend to us. Let's praise Jehovah for this and keep seeking Him out. Shalom!

Additional Inspiration: Psalm 119:5–6

Rx: Today be better than you were yesterday and tomorrow better than you are today. ~Dr. J

February 25

Proverb 25:6-7
Exalt

This Proverb teaches us to be humble and to check our arrogance factor. Self-esteem is a good thing, but arrogance and overconfidence is a trap. We must learn to read a room and read the people there. It is important we learn to blend first rather than exalt our self to a place of importance. If we remember that everyone has value in the eyes of our Lord, we may keep from making this mistake. Humility comes before honor. Be blessed!

Additional Inspiration: Psalm 149:4

February 26

Proverb 26:6
Fool

The only way to describe the first line of this Proverb is crazy, chaotic, and immobilizing. So, to put it frankly, if you want the job done, don't hire foolish people. They aren't dependable and they will drive you batty. What is unfortunate is the fact that you don't always know this about a person upfront. People often hide who they are at first.

If you are in a hiring position, reference checks and working interviews are key. In personal relationships we must also be careful of in whom we place our trust and dependence. Pray God brings upright people in your life personally and professionally. Amen!

Additional Inspiration: Psalm 49:1–3

Rx: Today be better than you were yesterday and tomorrow better than you are today. ~Dr. J

February 27

Proverb 27:2
Praise

This Proverb is an anti-twenty-first century culture message. We are living in the "I-century" during which our eye is on ourselves and our accomplishments. Our culture teaches us to be proud of who we are, to stand up for our rights, and to exercise our freedom of speech. It is quite easy for us to get caught in this web of likes, followers, praise, and honor. Some of us have become walking résumés. Let's pray that God helps us to remain humble all of our days. When we live right with Him, He gives us favor with Him and other people. Amen!

Additional Inspiration: Psalm 115:1

February 28

Proverb 28:3
Driving

This Proverb describes one who is extremely powerful in their position. A driving rain that leaves no crops destroys life and productivity. The crop provides food to the family and families of the community as well as providing income to the family who owns the farm. A ruler who oppresses kills those who they hold back. They do this by destroying their mind and body and breaking their spirit. Praise God that these rulers will face justice and receive their due penalty when Jehovah comes back to judge the people of the earth. Always keep hope in the forefront!

Additional Inspiration: Psalm 69:33

MARCH

Trust in the Lord with all your heart and lean not on your own understanding; in all your ways acknowledge him and he will make your paths straight.

Proverb 3:5-6

March 1

Proverb 1:5
Discerning

Dear friend, we can and do grow in knowledge and wisdom. This is not something exclusively for those who can afford it. The ability to gain insight is available to all and even more so to those who love God and intentionally pursue His purpose for their life. To sweeten the deal, Yahweh offers us this gift free of monetary charge.

However, we do pay with our time and effort. Obtaining wisdom is not convenient like a vending machine. On the contrary, we have to pray, read, write, meditate, and discuss with others in communion. When we do, God is faithful to give us this gift. Let us keep this in prayer today. Shalom!

Additional Inspiration: Psalm 90:12

March 2

Proverb 2:6
Understanding

When we consider this verse, it is clear that Jehovah is not hiding from us how to go about attaining wisdom. Do away with the "that's easier said than done" motto because it really is quite simple. Friends, we literally go to Him! You ask, "What does that look like in action?" Stop right now and imagine yourself in prayer, with a genuine heart, merely asking God for wisdom.

It can be as simple as "Abba Father, please bless me with your wisdom, infuse me with your thoughts." He promises us that from His mouth will come the knowledge and understanding we need. Trust—God's got this!

Additional Inspiration: Psalm 119:100

Rx: Today be better than you were yesterday and tomorrow better than you are today. ~Dr. J

March 3

Proverb 3:5
Trust

This verse is the quintessential pivotal point of spiritual growth. As hard as it is to completely wrap our fantastically crafted minds around it, we must learn to accept that we don't always have all the information. There are simply things we don't know, can't know, and will never know. When the situation doesn't make sense to our senses, we must remember what the Lord says: "My thoughts are higher than your thoughts and my ways are higher than your ways." We must continue daily prayer with God, reading His word and seeking council. He will give us the peace that transcends understanding. Trust and believe it!

Additional Inspiration: Psalm 25:1–2

March 4

Proverb 4:5
Swerve

"Don't forget" and "don't swerve" are crucial orders. Consider your job functions at work for a moment. As an employee you aim to stay on point. It doesn't look good when you forget to send an email or follow up with a client. Can one swerve professionally and expect to achieve the same results as one who hadn't veered off course? Only by God's grace! The recommendation given in this Proverb seems simple, but we have to choose not to swerve on a daily basis. Shalom!

Additional Inspiration: Psalm 139:17–18

March 5

Proverb 5:6
Crooked

The Lord describes for us someone living the carefree lifestyle. Sometimes that choice appears very desirable. Satan will tempt us with what looks promising and even tells us it is easier. Perhaps it is not overly sinful, so we feel right in our flesh. This is where awareness and real self-talk collide for our benefit. Remember, even Jesus was tempted in areas that were seemingly sinless.

So, it's not wrong to face temptation. It's what we do with it and how we act upon it. We mustn't deceive ourselves. As long as we are still breathing, we have time to make right what we know is wrong. It's time to get off the crooked path and start giving more thought to our way. Look up! Do you see God smiling? :-)

Additional Inspiration: Psalm 7:14

Rx: Today be better than you were yesterday and tomorrow better than you are today. ~Dr. J

March 6

Proverb 6:9
Sluggard

Some mornings I push my snooze button three times before I fully convince myself to rise from my slumber and get my day going. When I do, this verse always comes to mind. Due to many factors, this "jumping out of the bed at the first alarm phenomenon" comes naturally for some and not so much for others. This is something we must put into practice. Yes, we need rest, but not excessive rest; this is indeed why we have the Sabbath. This verse is warning us against being mentally, physically, and emotionally lazy. Are we the walking dead? Or are we alive? Live blessed because you are.

Additional Inspiration: Psalm 63:6–8

March 7

Proverb 7:3
Bind

From the inside out and from the outside in, the word of God is alive. It is life-changing, life-giving, and life-saving wisdom at our fingertips. Since we can understand what binding something means, imagine binding the word of God to your fingers. You can easily envision the deep level of familiarity He wants us have with the Bible. We are undergoing spiritual surgery. Meditation combined with prayer is our anesthesia and allows Jehovah time to operate on our hearts. Be blessed as you continue on your daily journey with Him. Shalom!

Additional Inspiration: Psalm 119:30–32

March 8

Proverb 8:8
Perverse

Dear friends, the words we speak have power, and the sooner we grasp of this concept, the better off we can be. We cannot and should not blurt out and speak "whatever" is on our minds. There is a way that is appropriate when we address one another. As followers of Christ and believers in Yahweh, we want to lean toward wholesome dialogue and allow only truth to leave our mouths.

Hold back on that off-color joke or perverted story. Think about it—those moments may make us laugh, but they do nothing to build us up in character. It can actually unconsciously affect our psychology and way of thinking in a negative way. Everything has an effect. Amen. So, let's think before we speak. Selah!

Additional Inspiration: Psalm 33:4

Rx: Today be better than you were yesterday and tomorrow better than you are today. ~Dr. J

March 9

Proverb 9:6
Simple

It is astounding to think that we, as awesome as a creation that we are, would be considered simple people. Simple in this sense is not a compliment; it's actually quite the opposite. God warns us to leave that mindset for good reason; we will live! When we walk in simple ways we are naïve, stupid, unintelligent, and easily fooled. Have you ever wondered why so many scammers scam so easily? Because we can be simple!

Yahweh wants to protect us from the perils of that way of living. His prescription is to walk in understanding. This means read the Scriptures, meditate on the word, pray and seek other counsel. Make every attempt to live right. There are rewards awaiting us. Shalom!

Additional Inspiration: Psalm 119:1–2

Rx: Today be better than you were yesterday and tomorrow better than you are today. ~Dr. J

March 10

Proverb 10:9
Integrity

Have you ever experienced working alongside someone who seems to have it easy or be really good at their work, only to later find out that they were gaming the system? This behavior happens all the time and is from the ancient days. Do not fret or tire of doing what is right. Ask yourself, doesn't Yahweh see them? Will they not have to give an account for their deeds? The answer is yes! Jehovah says they will come to ruin. Although it is disheartening to witness, trust God and know that as long as you are walking with integrity you can rest in the security of God's promise. Selah!

Additional Inspiration: Psalm 41:12

March 11

Proverb 11:10
Prosper

Dear friends, we cannot separate ourselves from community because communities are made up of a collection of individuals. When we realize that we all play a significant part in this life production, it can change our perspective and in turn our actions. This Proverb teaches us that it is right to want a healthy, prosperous community with clean air, safe water, affordable housing, job options, and excellent educational systems. We as a collective of individuals working together can attain all these good things when we walk the right path.

We all have witnessed personal and community destruction at the hands of those who are greedy, wicked, and unwise. Pray for personal and corporate leadership across the world. Look for ways to serve your community and do your part as an individual. Continue to ask God to let His will be done on earth as it is in Heaven. Blessings to you!

Additional Inspiration: Psalm 45:7

March 12

Proverb 12:3
Established

While it may look bleak as you watch the news and see the cray cray things happening around the world, we must remember who is in charge. We serve Jehovah Jireh, the king of all creation. The Alpha the Omega, the uncreated Creator—He's got it. Yes, over time many divisive families and people have seen earthly riches, but according to this Proverb, and throughout the Scriptures, evil is not rewarded. It is also not permanent and will ultimately be destroyed. So don't focus on the negative, because it's being handled—focus on what is right and your call to action. Your purpose and your legacy will be firmly established and will not be removed. Hallelujah!

Additional Inspiration: Psalm 103:17–19

Rx: Today be better than you were yesterday and tomorrow better than you are today. ~Dr. J

March 13

Proverb 13:4
Sluggard

Have you ever desired something but didn't want to work for it? Especially once you realized all the effort you would have to put out and all the energy you would have to expend. Yahweh ensures when we put forth our effort, and extend our energy in pursuing our calling, dreams, and goals, He will reward us. In fact, He says we will be "fully satisfied."

The opposite is also a guarantee. When we slug out and practice laziness, we get nothing. It seems like a straightforward, easy process to follow. Praise Yahweh and keep the fire burning in your heart. Use the energy of the heat to propel you forward. Shalom!

Additional Inspiration: Psalm 145:19

March 14

Proverb 14:10
Joy

Have you ever shared exciting news with someone only to find they didn't share your same enthusiasm? What about disappointment? Have you ever had someone tell you, "It's not that serious," only to leave you feeling silly for being upset and vulnerable? This Proverb highlights these exact types of scenarios. The truth is that God has put within each of us a joy and contentment that only we can fully appreciate. Likewise, our response to painful or stressful experiences is unique to each of us. We can't expect that others will share in these emotional states with us, but we can hope for their empathy. Be blessed and enjoy!

Additional Inspiration: Psalm 71:20–23

March 15

Proverb 15:4
Healing

Hallelujah, you don't have to be a doctor to be a healer. This Proverb highlights how powerful our speech is. Each of us has the gift of bringing healing to one another by the words we choose to speak. Likewise, we have the power to crush another person's spirit by the words we speak. This can be spoken directly to them, about them, or posted in social spaces.

We are walking around with an appendage that doubles as a weapon for evil and a wand for good. As much as we want to believe it, we do not have freedom of speech. It's more like freedom to censor our speech. Let's focus on speaking life into ourselves and into those around us. Shalom!

Additional Inspiration: Psalm 56:3–4

March 16

Proverb 16:3
Commit

Yahweh has a plan and purpose for each and every one of us. If you don't know what your purpose is, that doesn't mean that you are without one. It could mean that you have not asked God to reveal it to you, or you do not realize that you are in the midst of it. In the Psalms God tells us that He knows the dreams and desires of our hearts. We don't have to wonder how He knows, as He is the very source of those desires. In fact, our success is His success because He is working out all things for the good of those who love Him. Trust and believe Jehovah for this. You will see success indeed. Amen!

Additional Inspiration: Psalm 31:5

March 17

Proverb 17:9
Offense

Where is the love? Bring the peace and I'll show you the love. Praise God for this teaching. Here again we have been commissioned to promote love and peace. Let's be P.A.L.s and let Peace And Love abound. We are constantly barraged with information, good and bad. Just turn on the news or go to work; this is what humans do. Family, friends, and strangers alike all have the power to offend and sometimes without even knowing it.

A wise person covers an offense, overlooks it. This is for their sake and the sake of the offender. Obviously we are not speaking of gross offenses, like murder, we are referring to everyday interactions between people. Challenge yourself to be more aware, filter your words, and forgive. Shalom!

Additional Inspiration: Psalm 116:5–6

Rx: Today be better than you were yesterday and tomorrow better than you are today. ~Dr. J

March 18

Proverb 18:5
Justice

We see this happen in the United States and around the world. The course of justice is easily perverted due to the sinful nature of humans and Satan. It happens at every socioeconomic level and across sectors. In some cases we fight for ourselves and earn the right to be redeemed in the eyes of men and women. While in other situations this is not the case, and justice does not prevail. Although God does not approve of this, it happens due to humans not being upright. We should take a personal oath and make every effort to be fair and objective in our dealings. Pray about everything and wait for Yah's instruction. Shalom!

Additional Inspiration: Psalm 140:12–13

March 19

Proverb 19:5
False

We can believe and trust that God is who He says He is. Sometimes we are in situations that cause us to doubt or to wonder where is God and where is justice. Especially when we have been falsely accused or lied to by another. Not only do feelings of anger and betrayal set in, but feelings of embarrassment and concern for your character arise as well. While we certainly cannot go back in time, our Heavenly Father can!

According to this verse, there will be a day of justice for those who lie and pour out falsities to get their way and manipulate others. Yahweh wants us to know that when people operate in that mode, it eventually catches up to them. Yes, it's hard to believe it when we don't see immediate justice, but trust God. Stand with dignity and don't go to that level. Shalom!

Additional Inspiration: Psalm 5:4–6

Rx: Today be better than you were yesterday and tomorrow better than you are today. ~Dr. J

March 20

Proverb 20:4
Sluggard

A sluggard is one who is lazy and unproductive. Although it may feel nice to slug around a time or two, it definitely doesn't warrant a chronic lifestyle choice. Laziness brings on many spiritual, physical, and mental problems. Not to mention financial! As this Proverb indicates, a lazy person doesn't want to work and therefore has nothing. Let's consider this principle in all areas of our lives. Do you see some areas where this applies?

Don't fool yourself into thinking that you have to settle for anything. Allow yourself to dream and think about the areas that Yahweh is calling you to grow. Throw off any sluggardly ways that are holding you back, and go after your goals. Your discipline will lead to a harvest ripe with the blessings Yahweh has waiting for you. Shalom!

Additional Inspiration: Psalm 34:9–10

Rx: Today be better than you were yesterday and tomorrow better than you are today. ~Dr. J

March 21

Proverb 21:5
Haste

Intentional hard work leads to a harvest. We study, we go to school, we take our exam, we pass the test, we graduate…and with our degree, we go get a job that will allow us to earn a living. The athlete who trains many hours, sometimes with a sore and exhausted body, is still able to play the game and win because of his or her spirit of determination. Success doesn't usually happen overnight, and when it does it can be short-lived.

A tree that bears fruit does so due to consistency in proper care and watering. Remember, haste makes waste. When we make decisions quickly and don't look at what we are getting into, we can create a worse situation for ourselves. Be diligent, plan, and be blessed. Amen!

Additional Inspiration: Psalm 37:23–24

Rx: Today be better than you were yesterday and tomorrow better than you are today. ~Dr. J

March 22

Proverb 22:4
Humility

This Proverb indeed is our magic formula for success! All those who want wealth, honor, and life: throw your hands in the air. These are precious blessings from Yahweh that we all would love an abundance of. The good news is that any person who believes and obeys Yahweh can obtain His favor and receive these gifts. We don't have to go to a fancy school and pay a large tuition fee. All we must do is pray and obey, seek and fear the Lord, practice humility and meditate on His word. Ask God to show you where you can apply this Proverb in your life. Shalom!

Additional Inspiration: Psalm 149:4

March 23

Proverb 23:6-8
Stingy

As an associate working for others, I have seen the extremes that one may go to in order to save a buck or two. While it is definitely wise to always be conscious of your household and business finances, we have to be aware of when we are out of balance. God doesn't want us to be stingy; He wants us to be stewards! He actually encourages and rewards generosity.

Be honest with yourself. Only you and Yahweh know if the thought of giving is pleasant or painful for you. If it is the latter, ask God to change your heart. Start giving in small ways and watch how He transforms your life. Shalom!

Additional Inspiration: Psalm 37:27–28

March 24

Proverb 24:6
Guidance

While most of us will never go into full physical combat as the military does, we do engage in mini battles. We face life-altering decisions and confront oddball circumstances. Paul taught that we are in a spiritual war with the principalities of high and low places, although it looks like we are wrestling with flesh. The key life principle to take away is to not rely solely on our own expertise.

When dealing with major life-changing events and uniquely challenging circumstances, seek counsel from trusted family, friends, and experts. Sometimes our Father speaks through others to us. Trust His methods of helping us to achieve victory. Shalom!

Additional Inspiration: Psalm 32:8–9

Rx: Today be better than you were yesterday and tomorrow better than you are today. ~Dr. J

March 25

Proverb 25:9–10
Betray

Dear friends, be careful what you do and say, and who you say it to. We don't have as much control over who is watching us with the advances in technology, home video systems, body cams, and the like. Our Creator wants us to maintain integrity at all times. We should be honest, but we should also be mindful of what has been told to us by others in confidence, avoiding betraying another.

Yahweh wants us to understand and respect boundaries in our social and familial relationships. Reference Proverbs 25:8 and 25:17 for more instruction on how to set boundaries and avoid gossip. Keep praying and setting aside time devoted to God. He is smiling. Be blessed!

Additional Inspiration: Psalm 12:1–2

March 26

Proverb 26:7
Proverb

Are we useless or not being used as designed? In Yahweh's eyes, it is the latter. True, not every person is for the Lord. Moreover, some humans don't have good intentions, so we have to be on guard. When people are foolish yet profess wisdom, it is ill-fitting and we usually see them as hypocrites. These problems are written for all of us, not just one group of people. We all can be hypocrites at times. Amen! Let's take time to pray that we don't be hypocritical fools. Get wisdom and get understanding, even if it costs you all you have. Shalom!

Additional Inspiration: Psalm 73:25–26

Rx: Today be better than you were yesterday and tomorrow better than you are today. ~Dr. J

March 27

Proverb 27:4
Jealousy

This is a word that we come across in the Bible often. This word we are told to not partake in the 10 Commandments. This word can't be isolated and put on a table, but its damaging effects are in full view for all to see. We don't talk much about the power of this negative emotion and its ability to destroy. But it doesn't make it any less toxic. Here again, we must get honest with our own self. We must deal with jealousy before it gets a hold of us and we make bad choices. Praise God that He understands, for He is jealous for us and He can and will help us overcome in this area. Stay prayed up!

Additional Inspiration: Psalm 109:1–3

March 28

Proverb 28:5
Justice

This explains why we see so much injustice in the world! There are simply evil human beings who want to pervert the course of justice. They are so corrupt in their thought processes that they don't understand justice. According to the Proverb, what is wrong is right in their mind's eye. Those of us who seek the Lord understand when someone has been misjudged, falsely accused, and not redeemed.

Whenever and wherever, we must speak up for those who cannot speak for or defend themselves. Ultimately we must be patient and allow God to do what He does best—that is, reset the course of the evildoers and redeem the innocent. Today pray for those who are waiting for justice and are being falsely accused. Amen!

Additional Inspiration: Psalm 33:5

March 29

Proverb 29:5
Flattery

We all love a compliment or two but when it is overdone, it gives an air of being disingenuous. We should all look for ways to give honest compliments to one another daily. Scriptures tell us to encourage and uplift one another and refresh one another. We should look for ways to honor one another out of truth, not falsehood.

When we compliment because we want to persuade or take advantage of another person, that is spreading a net for that person's feet. They believe the other person's sincerity and become vulnerable. The outcomes can be good or bad. Be sensitive to the powerful tool of flattery and use it wisely. Shalom!

Additional Inspiration: Psalm 78:36–37

Rx: Today be better than you were yesterday and tomorrow better than you are today. ~Dr. J

March 30

Proverb 30:5
Flawless

Meditate for a moment and ponder the idea of flawlessness. We think of it easily from a beauty standpoint, but when we consider this from a spiritual lens, we should be even more enamored. For Yahweh's word to be flawless, it has to be truth without blemish. It has to be pure, honest, trustworthy, and reliable. For it to be a shield, it must be powerful, stable, and sound. The Bible, or as some call it, "Basic Instructions Before Leaving Earth," is all that and more. God left us His word as a way to connect with Him and others. Let's thank God for this spiritual textbook and praise Him for His trustworthy nature and protection. Amen!

Additional Inspiration: Psalm 32:7

Rx: Today be better than you were yesterday and tomorrow better than you are today. ~Dr. J

March 31

Proverb 31:10
Noble

Our character defines who we are and what we stand for. To be of noble character means you possess characteristics that are good, excellent, and noteworthy, such as generosity, honesty, and integrity. These are qualities any man or woman should want to acquire. In a world that appears to be leaning less on a moral foundation, it is important that we remind ourselves daily of the type of person we want to be and then walk in line with those qualities we have identified. Realize that by taking this journey with God, you are a rare jewel. Be blessed!

Additional Inspiration: Psalm 145:9

APRIL

There is a way that seems right to a man,
but in the end it leads to death.
                             Proverb 14:12

April 1

Proverb 1:7
Fear

We must learn to be careful what we wish for. Sometimes we want the wrong things for our lives because we lack the foresight and knowledge of God. Knowledge can get us in trouble, but it can also be life-saving. Wanting to know more is what got Adam and Eve in the predicament that affected the rest of humanity. We must listen to and obey our Creator as He instructs us. If we want knowledge and wisdom, then we must develop a healthy fear of Yahweh. We must not be afraid of His loving discipline and make efforts to live a disciplined life. Be blessed, my friend!

Additional Inspiration: Psalm 103:11

April 2

Proverb 2:7
Shield

Hallelujah! Praise God for this promise. Yes to victory and yes to the protection of the Father of Heavenly Lights. Don't think for one minute that this covenant doesn't apply to you. When you accepted Jesus as your savior, His death covered all your sins. In Jehovah's eyes, when we accept His son, seek His will, and apply what we learn to our lives, we are living upright.

We stand blameless! Yes, we may mess up from time to time, but we repent and move on. God's got our back and will be our shield. He has big plans for you, so keep believing and running your race. Shalom!

Additional Inspiration: Psalm 34:19

Rx: Today be better than you were yesterday and tomorrow better than you are today. ~Dr. J

April 3

Proverb 3:6
Acknowledge

When we take time to acknowledge someone, we are bringing them into the mix, looping them in, so to speak, and making them part of the circle. It is an action on the part of the acknowledger, not the person to be acknowledged. Every day that we wake and are able to breathe, Yah is acknowledging us. Likewise, we must take the time to intentionally honor God.

Nothing is hidden from Jehovah, for He knows everything about us. He speaks His way, through creation and Jesus's work on the cross. What He desires from us is relationship. God wants us to surrender our desires, hopes, and dreams to His will. He can respond by giving us a clear mind to make sound decisions that open up doors and opportunities. Our relationship with Him allows us to make our journey with a few less detours. Shalom!

Additional Inspiration: Psalm 25:4

Rx: Today be better than you were yesterday and tomorrow better than you are today. ~Dr. J

April 4

Proverb 4:6
Wisdom

Yahweh admonishes us to not let wisdom out of our sight. We are taught that not forsaking something or someone means to not turn away from it and to not turn your back on the person. To forsake wisdom would render it ineffective in our life. Why would we want to turn off our spiritual alarm system? We invest in home alarms and security systems to protect our things and us. Our choices need guidance. We learn in this Proverb that wisdom watches over us and protects us. Let's activate her, shall we?

Additional Inspiration: Psalm 37:30–31

April 5

Proverb 5:7
Listen

This goes for both sons and daughters: listen up. Yahweh urges us to pay attention and to not forget what we learn. In order for us to become one with the Scriptures, we must commit to reading them daily. We must pray and ask God to show us and teach us what He wants us to know as we read and reflect on His word. When we take it a step further and actively listen, we can put pen to paper what He speaks to our heart and review it again later. As we operate in that spiritual cycle, we learn and grow. God smiles and blessings flow. Shalom!

Additional Inspiration: Psalm 81:13–16

April 6

Proverb 6:10–11
Scarcity

We are encouraged to not be lazy, oversleep, and get too much rest. Yahweh worked six days and rested a full Sabbath day. Ecclesiastes 11:6 instructs us to sow our seed in the morning and to not let our hands be idle at night. For we don't know which will be a success—whether this, that, or both will do equally well. Our sure way to poverty is laziness. When we have a lazy mind and body, we leave ourselves open to disease, poverty, and destruction. Let us remain dedicated to living an active life. Live blessed because you are!

Additional Inspiration: Psalm 90:17

April 7

Proverb 7:4
Kinsman

As you read the Scriptures, notice the frequency of the action of spoken word. It is powerful! Yahweh intelligently spoke creation and design into existence. Wisdom and understanding were His accomplices in all we see. Made in the image of God Most High, we must realize that we have the same ability to intelligently create and design. We must activate that power that dwells within us.

We can do what we set our mind to and say we can do. Just like our Creator, we must have our accomplices, our kinsman. Good thing all we have to do is call, and the omniscient mind of God will provide all the wisdom and understanding that we need. Amen!

Additional Inspiration: Psalm 119:24

April 8

Proverb 8:10–11
Instruction

As appealing as all the glitz and glam is, none of it compares to the knowledge of God and a true and active relationship with Him. Yahweh makes a bold statement in this Proverb that none of the most beautiful stones, gems, and jewels that He has made compare to His instruction. Many of us hated to be told what to do by our parents or other authority. This attitude leads many teens and young adults to make foolish decisions in the heat of a rebellious mindset.

The bad consequences that accompany our foolish decisions are never well-received, and we end up with the "woe is me" complex. We are always children of God, and we will always need His guidance. This is the very reason He sent the Holy Spirit. Continue learning The Way, praying for wisdom and leaning into God. When we do this, we will be blessed. Amen!

Additional Inspiration: Psalm 119:72

Rx: Today be better than you were yesterday and tomorrow better than you are today. ~Dr. J

April 9

Proverb 9:7
Mocker

Dear friend, don't be afraid to share your faith and speak boldly the word you have been taught. Remember, iron sharpens iron, and we help each other improve. Of course, there are many people who do not believe in God, in addition to those who believe but want to live in antithesis to The Way. So prepare yourself for pushback from those who fit the description of mocker or wicked. Simply knowing that you can and will meet resistance is half the battle and makes it a little easier to be bold. Trust that God will give you the words, strength, and protection in all situations. Amen!

Additional Inspiration: Psalm 64:1-6

April 10

Proverb 10:11
Fountain

The book of James states that the tongue is the smallest part of the body but has the power to destroy. We ought to take some time to really consider this truth and the good and bad consequences that come with the responsibility of being a tongue owner. How do we challenge ourselves to only speak life, love, encouragement, promotion, and edification? Should we never express our anger? Friends, we must find balance. That is the key.

Yahweh gave us emotions as a healthy way to communicate, but we must use wisdom and show restraint at all times. Stay away from violent people and those seeking to conduct evil. Keep peace in your body, mind, relationships, and homes. Be the fountain of life that you are called to be. Amen!

Additional Inspiration: Psalm 40:3

Rx: Today be better than you were yesterday and tomorrow better than you are today. ~Dr. J

April 11

Proverb 11:12
Derides

When we deride another person, we are being critical, insulting, or bitter toward them. When we think or say someone is ridiculous, has no value, or when we laugh and make fun of someone, that is a form of deriding our neighbor. If you ever had this happen to you, then you know firsthand that it is embarrassing and depressing.

Of course we should learn not to be too sensitive, but we also have a responsibility as humans to be mindful of what we say and how we are saying it. My friends, holding our tongue is paramount, and this becomes increasingly clear the more you read the Proverbs and other scriptures. Let's pray on this and make a daily conscious effort to censor our speech. Shalom!

Additional Inspiration: Psalm 101:7

April 12

Proverb 12:11
Abundant

We reap what we sow! A person who invests their time working toward concrete goals will one day attain them. Our Creator has woven desires of our heart into the fabric of our DNA. The Scriptures are laden with the verses promising to give us the desires of our heart.

When our dreams align with God's plans for us and we sow seed in those areas, in due time, we enter into an abundant harvest. When our desires are not in line with God's plans for us, we end up chasing fantasies that lead us on unproductive paths, including poverty. Let's focus our energy and pray to stay aligned with Yah's will for our lives. Get ready for your overflow season. Selah!

Additional Inspiration: Psalm 20:4

Rx: Today be better than you were yesterday and tomorrow better than you are today. ~Dr. J

April 13

Proverb 13:7
Pretend

Don't judge a book by its cover and don't trust everything you see and hear. It may not be what it seems. This is what the Proverb teaches us. It is so easy for us as humans to put on fronts for ourselves and for others. And while we may fool each other from time to time, we never fool God. We should not be afraid to be who we are, but we must remember to show humility and not let arrogance and prestige lead us astray.

Sometimes we feel we need to "keep up with the Joneses" to fit in, but we lead ourselves down a perilous trail if we follow this worldly philosophy. Put off your old self—don't pattern yourself after this world. Be the unique you that you are and follow Yeshua. Amen!

Additional Inspiration: Psalm 121:1–2

Rx: Today be better than you were yesterday and tomorrow better than you are today. ~Dr. J

April 14

Proverb 14:12
Seems

This Proverb reads so clear that there is no need for word dissection. It clearly highlights our profound need for wisdom and discernment and the strength to act on both in our lives. Stop now and reflect on the verse, "There is a way that seems right." What in your life seems right but you know it really may not be? The answer to that question is the exact area where Yahweh wants to have His way!

Of course we cannot ultimately avoid death. However, what this Proverb really speaks to is the untimely deaths, early deaths, death of passions, death of dreams, death of hope, death of relationships and death of well-being. This Proverb is a wake-up call to develop and maintain healthy life habits and live with purpose. Keep reading the word, meditating on it, and dialoguing with Jehovah. Be blessed!

Additional Inspiration: Psalm 119:48

Rx: Today be better than you were yesterday and tomorrow better than you are today. ~Dr. J

April 15

Proverb 15:9
Ways

It's all about our intentions, the posture of our heart. This is what God is after. He knows the seed we descend from. Yahweh is not asking us to be perfect all at once. He is taking us from glory to glory through a lifetime process of transformation. What feels long to us is a blink to Him. Our charge is to follow and pursue Him in the way of righteousness every day in all we do.

Yes, we will stumble. Yes, we will fall. Yes, we will think we are making no progress at all. Accept that these thoughts may come from the enemy, but don't give up and go down in defeat. Choose wisely and monitor your intentions. God uses our circumstances to make us stronger. Amen!

Additional Inspiration: Psalm 99:4

April 16

Proverb 16:7
Enemy

Believe it or not, you might be someone's enemy. Even the nicest things about us can get on someone's nerves. God makes us a promise in this Proverb that is crucial for experiencing peace during our days on Earth. So long as we have to interact with people, it is desirable to have peace-filled relationships.

Days, weeks, months ripe with interactions filled with dissension and quarreling are draining on our physical, mental, and spiritual realms. As highly sought after as it is, most of us wish we could buy peace, but we cannot. So it is truly a blessing from God when we have true peace. Shalom!

Additional Inspiration: Psalm 56:10–11

Rx: Today be better than you were yesterday and tomorrow better than you are today. ~Dr. J

April 17

Proverb 17:10
Rebuke

Dear Lord, forgive us we are hard-headed, but we don't mean it. We all know people who just can't seem to catch a break. Bad stuff always happens to them. You may be in a situation where you have suffered the hundred plus lashes in the form of gross negative consequences, yet you still commit the same action or similar actions. Do you wonder when you will learn or when God will have His way with you?

God tells us that when we actually achieve a level of mature enlightenment, wisdom will impress us. Constructive criticism, recommendations, suggestions, and rebukes will actually call our attention in a good way, and we will want to change our actions, thoughts, behaviors, and emotions. Pray for a discerning spirit, because Adonai wants to give it to us. Amen!

Additional Inspiration: Psalm 92:5–7

Rx: Today be better than you were yesterday and tomorrow better than you are today. ~Dr. J

April 18

Proverb 18:8
Gossip

We are living in the tech age where info is literally at our fingertips. We can easily stay up to date on the latest dish. Whether it be famous people, friends, or coworkers, it feels good to be in the loop and to have the scoop. Those few words, "I shouldn't be telling you this but…" seem to make our ears tickle with glee. Tread lightly here. As we grow in our faith, we must learn that God only wants what is good for us. Gossiping breeds negative consequences, so always think before you repeat, think before you listen, and think before you speak. Shalom!

Additional Inspiration: Psalm 15:1–3

April 19

Proverb 19:8
Cherish

Love your mind! There is so much richness within this verse, but two themes stand out from the pages. The first is our responsibility to lead a life with a sound mind. Well, what does that look like exactly? How does that concept manifest? The first step is to get wisdom.

We obtain wisdom via prayer, reading scripture and other books, seeking advice from sage counsel, watching educational videos, and meditation. These actions put us in a position to get knowledge that we don't already have. When we cherish something, we hold it near to us and we treat it tenderly. When we decide to cherish our mind, we will naturally want to protect it and not pollute it with toxins (i.e. bad thoughts, images, etc.).

We want to feed it healthy thoughts and images. We want to keep it clean and exercise it by learning and doing new things. This is prosperity in action, the promise given to us by Jehovah. Now walk it out and be blessed!

Additional Inspiration: Psalm 119:73

Rx: Today be better than you were yesterday and tomorrow better than you are today. ~Dr. J

April 20

Proverb 20:5
Purpose

Many of us feel like we don't know our purpose or our calling. Often times it is because we compare ourselves to people who confess they knew their calling at two years of age or those who are genuinely passionate about one major thing and pursue it with everything they have. Rule No. 1: Don't compare ourselves amongst ourselves. Jesus is our standard, Amen. According to this verse, God designed us all with poly-purpose. We are not just called for one thing.

Every role you fill is a place of purpose for you. When you walk with God, feel free to ask Him for wisdom and knowledge of His plan for your life. Then you are better able to make decisions and follow your dreams. Pray, trust, and believe it! Shalom.

Additional Inspiration: Psalm 138:8

Rx: Today be better than you were yesterday and tomorrow better than you are today. ~Dr. J

April 21

Proverb 21:13
Poor

Give freely! We should never be afraid to give to those in need. Please don't think Yah will strike you down and not answer your prayer because you don't give to everyone you see. God is trying to teach to have a heart of service toward others and a giving spirit. God loves a cheerful giver! God is warning us to not be stingy with our time, talents, and resources.

We reap what we sow. If we simply withhold generosity just because, generosity by spiritual laws cannot be returned to us unless Yah overrules it. Let's meditate on this and ask God to turn up our generosity. Every day is a good day to give. Shalom!

Additional Inspiration: Psalm 37:25–26

April 22

Proverb 22:5
Snare

No more drama! Yahweh never promised us a problem-free life. In fact, Jesus told us that we would have trials and tribulations in this life. However, those who love Yah and have accepted Jesus as savior have the same ability as Jesus to triumph and overcome adversity. Make no mistake though, God tells us very plainly, if we go seek for trouble, we will surely find it. If we sow wickedness, wicked actions and thoughts, we will indeed reap a life of turmoil and negativity.

Snares and thorns will forever be in the path of those who are evil. If this sounds undesirable to you, praise because that is not the life Jehovah intends for us who have been called in Yeshua. Guard your soul, my friend, with everything you have. Protect your mind and heart. Then you will have the peace and ability to overcome the tests in your life. Shalom!

Additional Inspiration: Psalm 62:1–2

Rx: Today be better than you were yesterday and tomorrow better than you are today. ~Dr. J

April 23

Proverb 23:12
Apply

This is a clear command and call for action! But how exactly does application work? When God asks us to apply our heart to instruction, He is asking us to allow His word to become our guide. He wants us to be intimate with the Scriptures, have them ready on our lips, so we can give sound answers. We must seek Him and His word daily. When ready, we must apply our ears to each word of knowledge and actively listen with the intention of learning. We can then access this wisdom when we need it, and it will be a guiding light to our feet. Amen!

Additional Inspiration: Psalm 27:4

April 24

Proverb 24:10
Falter

If you suffer from small strength, please refer to Proverb 24:5. Meditate on that verse and ask God to help you increase in wisdom and knowledge. During difficult times, we must remember that Yahweh is allowing us an opportunity to grow. No one can explain why we get dealt the card we get. Sometimes it appears unfair, but the best thing to remember is that the same God gets us through it all.

Easier said than done, true. But, really make an effort to not let your circumstances dictate your faith. It may seem uncomfortable at first, but the next time you find yourself in a time of trouble, pray and actually thank God for the trial and ask Him to show you His wisdom for the situation. He promises to never forsake us and to not put more on us than we can bear. What a good-good father. Amen!

Additional Inspiration: Psalm 69:29–31

Rx: Today be better than you were yesterday and tomorrow better than you are today. ~Dr. J

April 25

Proverb 25:11
Aptly

Psychologists have studied a phenomenon termed "odd man out" syndrome, which describes that the mind of man naturally discriminates differences in the environment out of a need for information, survival, and communication. We are fearlessly and wonderfully made, Amen! Yahweh designed us to notice differences. He enabled us to see when something stands out with this cleverly crafted feature.

Jehovah also demonstrates strength through timely spoken word. All of creation exists via logos. A word spoken quickly, effectively, and with purpose stands out and is transformative. This should encourage us to use our same God-given gift of spoken word to bring change to the people and world around us. Shalom!

Additional Inspiration: Psalm 5:3

April 26

Proverb 26:8
Fool

Danger, danger, danger—a stone tied in a sling is dangerous and obviously unable to support the weight. Likewise, when honor is given to a fool, it is dangerous, and the fool cannot support the weight that comes with such title or respect. Just like the stone in a sling, it becomes hard to manage the load. Pray that we do not remain in our folly so when honor comes looking for us we can be ready to receive with grace. Amen!

Additional Inspiration: Psalm 53:2–3

April 27

Proverb 27:6
Friend

Like me! In our current technologically savvy era, we make friends so easily. We are excited for likes, tweets, re-tweets, and followers. The notion of being popular has taken a different form, and while all the social interaction has its pros, the cons are ever-present. More people than before are lonely, and suicide rates have increased. The truth is we cannot be friends with everyone.

Sometimes there are people we don't care for, and likewise we don't tickle their fancy, either. Yes, those who we are close to can and will hurt us from time to time. Simultaneously, an enemy can easily deceive you by buttering you up in the presence of others. Be on guard as this Proverb dictates. One thing that never fails is taking time to get to know people. Pray for God to bring the right friends into your life. Amen!

Additional Inspiration: Psalm 18:3,6

Rx: Today be better than you were yesterday and tomorrow better than you are today. ~Dr. J

April 28

Proverb 28:11
Discernment

Dear friend, it doesn't matter what level of socioeconomic status that God has placed us. One thing we all have in common is He has given us a mind to think and a spirit with which to commune with Him. When we pray and invite God to lead our lives, we shouldn't focus our energy worrying about be taken advantage of.

Yeshua tells us to not live with anxiety and to cast our cares on Him. He wants to protect us from those, who being wise in their own eyes, desire to lead us into a situation or trap for their benefit. This is why Yahweh teaches us to pray about everything. Present all your petitions to Him, friends. We serve a God who cares, a God of action, and a God of justice. Be blessed today!

Additional Inspiration: Psalm 107:41–43

Rx: Today be better than you were yesterday and tomorrow better than you are today. ~Dr. J

April 29

Proverb 29:7
Justice

We see this Proverb played out daily on our streets, in the paper, on TV, and on the Internet. There are so many people in the world with so much unmet need. Some choose not to believe in God because of the persistent evil, natural disasters, and economic disparities they see. They exclaim, "There cannot be a God. Why would a loving God let this happen? Millions of innocents have died." Unfortunately, they shake their fist at the wrong being and don't understand God's ways.

Humans with sinful intentions and the powers of darkness are to blame for much of the destruction and inequities. God gave us dominion to rule on earth. We are His hands and feet, and we have the whole earth full of resources. As this Proverb indicates, certain types of humans have no such concern about justice and they clog and pervert the system. The least we can do is our part and leave the rest to God. He's got it! Shalom.

Additional Inspiration: 29:7

Rx: Today be better than you were yesterday and tomorrow better than you are today. ~Dr. J

April 30

Proverb 30:6
Rebuke

We can trust in the word of Yah! The Bible is a collection of sixty-six books with forty authors that tell a similar story over periods of time, and all reflect the One True God, Yahweh. In order to take our spiritual walk from glory to glory, we must learn to read, meditate on, and trust the word of God. This is a crucial part of our growth experience.

What we say matters, and most of us are bothered when someone "twists our words." Many arguments contain the phrases "That's not what I said" or "That's not what I meant." Our Creator feels the same way when we attempt to alter or edit His word. Be careful of various translations, and always pray before studying. Continue learning and be blessed. Shalom!

Additional Inspiration: Psalm 12:6

May

From the fruit of his lips a man is filled with good things as surely as the work of his hands rewards him.

> Proverb 12:14

May 1

Proverb 1:10
Entice

Dear friends, we must be careful and not deceive ourselves. No matter our age, we are susceptible to persuasion and peer pressure. Adults are not immune to influence. If we were not easily convinced or enticed, the advertising sector would not have the staying power or profitable effect we see that it has.

Sometimes we want to just go along with the crowd to get along and not seem like the odd person out, little knowing that we can and will eventually be like the company we keep. Be cautious of your surroundings as well as whom you are surrounded by. Pray and make healthy decisions. Shalom abounding!

Additional Inspiration: Psalm 141:4

May 2

Proverb 2:9
Path

Dear friend, there are many ways that seem right to us but in the end lead to heartache, regret, and death. Set before all are well-lit paths and dim and dark alleys, good and bad ways to walk in alike. It is imperative that we grasp this truth as we proceed on our journey of life, because it can save us from unnecessary trouble.

Think about the kind of life you desire to live and the type of person you desire to be. Yah tells us that with wisdom we will understand how to "walk the talk." We should desire to uphold what is right, just, and fair. Be bold to walk out your own unique path of greatness. Pray, stay active, and be blessed!

Additional Inspiration: Psalm 89:14–15

Rx: Today be better than you were yesterday and tomorrow better than you are today. ~Dr. J

May 3

Proverb 3:7–8
Shun

Dear friend, there are many people and activities clamoring for our attention and participation. For some of us this creates a feeling of adventure and excitement, while others may feel intimidated or overwhelmed by too much stimulus. If given a choice, would you prefer to be a robot preprogrammed to think, speak, and act, or would you prefer the freedom that you have now, to think, speak, and act for yourself? The answer may seem obvious, yet it is this very human birthright that has brought endless peril and disaster in our world.

The choices we make always come with immediate and or long-term consequences, whether good or bad. No doubt trouble can come our way when we don't expect it or deserve it. However, we can always willfully choose to avoid evil, which inevitably leads to destruction. Let's spend some time meditating on this and consider the choices we make in every aspect of our lives. Pray God enables you to stay aligned with Him. Be blessed!

Additional Inspiration: Psalm 111:10

May 4

Proverb 4:7
Supreme

There is something inherent in the individual and a collection of individuals that enjoys the feeling of being number one. This joy is easily observed when one wins a Nobel Peace Prize or a team wins the Super Bowl, for example. To be supreme, the highest, and best is what many men and women strive for personally and professionally, on and off the court.

It costs us in time and money to be the supreme Olympic athlete, dentist, physician, lawyer, businessperson, pastor, parent, teacher, or any other profession. To be top of the rank is work, but it is worth it when we receive the benefits. In this same light is how we must approach wisdom and understanding. We must attain them at any and all costs. It is well worth the time invested for the rewards they offer. Amen!

Additional Inspiration: Psalm 119:72

Rx: Today be better than you were yesterday and tomorrow better than you are today. ~Dr. J

May 5

Proverb 5:10-11
Toil

Dear friend, for some of us it is hard to take heed when we hear warnings. Sometimes we think, "Oh, that doesn't apply to me; that's for those people." The truth is we are all sinners and have fallen short of the glory of God. Amen for Yeshua's work on the cross because we are indeed redeemed. However, we are still held accountable for our actions.

When we partner with the evil side, with people who are wicked in their ways, we can bet there will be consequences. Whether it is disease, bad breaks, fines, penalties, child support, alimony, and so on, we pay a price for our bad choices. We will toil and make another person comfortable while our bodies get worn out and used up. Dear friends, let's pray that we not be wise in our own eyes and stay far from the path of evil. Continuously consider our ways and motives and be refined daily. Be blessed!

Additional Inspiration: Psalm 128:1-2

May 6

Proverb 6:15
Overtake

We need to understand the type of God we serve. We serve a God who avenges on behalf of those who love Him. He is not content with evil even though it is persistent around us. He is watching and He is constantly extending grace. We have all sinned and fallen short of the glory of God; however, those who accept Christ and make an effort to be right with God in our daily living don't need to live in fear of being suddenly overtaken and destroyed. Yahweh is warning us how not to live and the ultimate consequence of our poor choices. Keep choosing to live right. Run your race without fear. Shalom!

Additional Inspiration: Psalm 119:104

May 7

Proverb 7:5
Wayward

Managing affairs of the heart and mind are an ongoing challenge. While some of us have not and may not encounter having an affair on a spouse or significant other, many of us have. We must always be on guard and be mindful of our actions and speech and that of others. If you are in a committed relationship, keep your distance from flirtatious and seductive relationships and environments. Remember, the adulteress takes on many forms. Be aware of yourself—guard your heart and mind. Shalom!

Additional Inspiration: Psalm 140:1–3

May 8

Proverb 8:12
Prudence

Dear friends, life as we all know has its ups and downs. No matter what we see on TV, in magazines, or on Facebook, no one has an absolute perfect life. We all encounter trials, doubts, fears, and uncertainties. True, some of us have a much more difficult experience than others, but we all experience.

What we do with our experiences and how we respond to them is the best method for building our character. This is also when we get to see God show up and show out in our life. No matter what season your life is in right now, seek the wisdom of God. Seek to live a disciplined life and apply what you learn. Yahweh sees and is pleased. Be blessed!

Additional Inspiration: Psalm 94:9–11

May 9

Proverb 9:8
Rebuke

We are never too old to learn. Praise God that He is so patient with us. It takes a long time for some of us to take a baby step of faith in any direction. Our Creator waits patiently, constantly wooing us to Him. When we pray, meditate, and remain open to listening to Him, Yahweh can do insanely awesome things in our lives. As adults we are still children to God, and as such, we are still correctable and teachable. Let's be wise and always consider our ways. Consider making it a point to improve daily. Shalom!

Additional Inspiration: Psalm 19:12–13

May 10

Proverb 10:14
Store

The theme of Proverbs 10 is fools and mouths. We need to learn spiritual and social mores and use them as guiding compasses. "Wise men store up knowledge" means that they hold onto it, save it, review it, and continue to learn more. When we store something we in essence preserve it for later use or consumption. That's the point of storing!

Yahweh wants us to store and retrieve knowledge to enable us to walk as He walked, in spiritual social elegance. Our freedom is in our faith and self-control. Choose our words wisely and speak life and love to people. Stay aware and be blessed!

Additional Inspiration: Psalm 119:43–44

May 11

Proverb 11:13
Trustworthy

Good friends can be hard to find and hard to hold onto, but they are worth the effort we put into the relationship. Trust between friends goes through phases similar to dating relationships. We must possess a certain level of vulnerability to open ourselves up to friendship. When we find genuine relationships, they may shift due to life circumstances, but in many situations they are well worth the effort to maintain. Think about one of your close trustworthy friends and thank God for them. Let them know next time you speak how much their friendship means to you. Shalom!

Additional Inspiration: Psalm 25:14

May 12

Proverb 12:14
Reward

Have you heard the saying, "You are what you say and do"? Well, God shows us very clearly in this Proverb that is true. Jehovah spoke and put our universe in motion. We are made in His image and have the same power to speak transformation into our world. God has given us the ability to speak blessings into our lives and to do work that brings profit. Our words have the power to speak life or death into ourselves and others.

We must use extreme caution when we speak and aim to use words that are encouraging, uplifting, loving, kind, and honest. Be careful to not be idle. Keep your hands busy at work. Yahweh promises to prosper us when we are obedient to His instruction. Let's practice and be blessed!

Additional Inspiration: Psalm 92:14–15

Rx: Today be better than you were yesterday and tomorrow better than you are today. ~Dr. J

May 13

Proverb 13:10
Pride

Dear friends, as you read Proverbs 13, take note of how often Yahweh tells us to heed instruction and take advice. Is there any question or doubt in your mind regarding the value or importance of these recommendations? When we think we know it all and can figure it out and don't need advice, we live from a place of pride and arrogance.

This is a dangerous space to operate within because it can lead to undesirable consequences. Think before speaking or acting. Some of us need to go so far to think before thinking. Things that make you go *hmmm*. Never be afraid or too proud to seek wise counsel. Be blessed!

Additional Inspiration: Psalm 138:6

May 14

Proverb 14:13
Grief

Have you ever experienced making up with someone you were mad at? Do you remember how your heart was badly hurt over the disagreement or betrayal? Do you remember when you had the opportunity to make amends with the other person? Maybe smiles were exchanged or a hug. Perhaps a handshake took place or a joke was exchanged to break the ice. Soon thereafter, the laughter, albeit awkward, appears.

No doubt, if feels good to be able to reestablish peace and harmony. Situations may shock us and send us on roller-coaster rides of grief, joy, aches, and laughter. As long as we know there will always be ups and downs in life and relationships, we will be able to use our faith to persevere through with the help of God. Shalom!

Additional Inspiration: Psalm 126:5–6

Rx: Today be better than you were yesterday and tomorrow better than you are today. ~Dr. J

May 15

Proverb 15:13
Cheerful

The condition of our heart is vital for our spiritual, mental, and physical life. Throughout Scriptures we are taught that the heart of humans reveals the true person. Therefore we must exercise and take care of our hearts. We feel a lot through this organ, Amen. By God's design a heart can beat on its own even once separated from the body. How amazing is that! Our heart has its own mind.

Our heart's condition can uplift us as well as others around us. It can also crush us, and others. Awareness of our heart is key to being mindful. Take care of yourself and remember: a happy heart = a cheerful face. Shalom!

Additional Inspiration: Psalm 42:11

May 16

Proverb 16:9
Plan

How often does this happen? You make plans to do this or that or to go here and there and you end up doing something completely different. Often times this change of plans wasn't even on our radar. In our daily lives we dream, plan, and calendar a variety of ideas and events. This is a good thing and helps encourage discipline and focus. However, Yahweh wants us to know that He is the ultimate decision maker when it comes to our life. If we ask for His will to be done in our lives, trust, and believe, He will give purpose to each step we take. Shalom!

Additional Inspiration: Psalm 85:13

May 17

Proverb 17:12
Folly

This sounds so crazy, chaotic, and scary. A bear robbed of her cubs. I don't think any of us besides our hunting friends desire to meet a bear, let alone one whose babies have been kidnapped. No, no, I'll pass. You? In comparison, meeting a human being classified as a fool reveling in their folly doesn't sound so bad. But according to Yahweh, the latter is worse.

Human beings doing foolish things have the ability to end lives on the magnitude of hundreds to thousands with a single inhumane act. Reflect on the recent U.S. school shootings, U.S. slave trade, civil rights movement, Holocaust, Rwanda genocide, 911, suicide bombers, and other terrorists acts, just to name a few. Yeah, so about that bear and her cubs…Shalom!

Additional Inspiration: Psalm 121:7-8

May 18

Proverb 18:9
Slack

Work, work, work, work, work, work! It seems like this is our life mantra. From Genesis humans were commissioned to toil. We can only consider it a blessing when our work aligns with our gifts, talents, and desires. Sometimes we don't like our job, but we know we need the money to survive. Although it may not be our dream job, we can still do it with a smile and give our best.

We should take our job seriously and be professional no matter what. This applies to all work, paid or volunteer. God compares laziness to partnering with the dark side, a destroyer, and that is extremely telling of how serious God is about this topic. Work hard and be blessed. Shalom!

Additional Inspiration: Psalm 18:9

May 19

Proverb 19:11
Glory

We are officially in a technological age where face-to-face encounters are not needed for communication. Good or bad, it is easy for some information to be lost in satellite translation. We may be left wondering what he or she meant due to their lack of detailed script. Truly it is hard to read between the lines. We don't have enough time or energy to confront every situation where this happens. Whether via text, in person, or through emails, if we are to be like Jesus, we are to aim for peace and love at all times. So next time you feel offended, stop and think, "If I overlook this, I will be glorified by God." Selah!

Additional Inspiration: Psalm 18:27

May 20

Proverb 20:13
Sleep

Dear friends, Yahweh warns us over and over again, throughout Scripture, about the perils of laziness. There is no joy and no productivity in sleeping your life away. Notice the scripture doesn't imply "maybe," it says "or," which is a guaranteed option of either this or that. There is evidence in the Bible that God wants us working most of the day.

Of course God wants us to get a healthy number of hours of sleep and refresh, but we should keep ourselves busy with the work the Lord gave us to do. This includes our job, education, volunteering, caring for family, nurturing friendships, prayer, meditation, and devotional time. When we tend to these areas of our lives and do it unto the Lord, we will surely see an abundant harvest. Shalom!

Additional Inspiration: Psalm 139:1–3

Rx: Today be better than you were yesterday and tomorrow better than you are today. ~Dr. J

May 21

Proverb 21:16
Straight

Yahweh teaches us that we have the choice to walk in light, to walk in darkness, or to waver in between. To God this wavering is referred to as being lukewarm, a position that is unfavorable to our Creator. We serve a God who is light and wants to illuminate all of us. When we choose to walk in the way of understanding, learn His ways, meditate on the Scriptures, pray, and apply what we learn, we experience the supernatural. God takes us from glory to glory on a fantastic voyage.

When we choose to walk in any other path that is not aligned with our Creator, we are in essence walking in the dark. There is no life in the dark, and that is where the dead rest. Don't waiver and waive your rights to an abundant life. Choose light, choose love, and choose Yahweh. Shalom!

Additional Inspiration: Psalm 119:7–8

Rx: Today be better than you were yesterday and tomorrow better than you are today. ~Dr. J

May 22

Proverb 22:7
Lender

It doesn't matter where you look, throughout the earth people organize themselves in the fashion described in this Proverb. Every country has a tiered socioeconomic system. In many cases a small percentage of the wealthy elite own most of the country.

Merchant business has always existed in some form of sales, bartering, trading, and loaning. Our current system leans heavily on financing, loans, and debt. This creates even more dependency of the poor on the wealthy. Hence they become a slave to the lender.

Freedom can elude us in many ways, and poor financial stewardship is one way we remain in bondage. Certainly, not all debt is bad, and some situations are beyond our control. However, we must first know the difference and then learn to live within or below our means. Shalom!

Additional Inspiration: Psalm 103:6

Rx: Today be better than you were yesterday and tomorrow better than you are today. ~Dr. J

May 23

Proverb 23:15-16
Joy

One surefire way to get our Jehovah to smile and rejoice is for us to be wise in our heart and to speak truth. God has given us the ability to do this; otherwise He wouldn't suggest it to us. We develop wisdom by seeking God. You are already on that track if you have picked up this book. Seek God with all your heart and mind. Pray for wisdom and understanding, because God promises to give it to us.

Please know that we don't serve a God who desires to trick us. We may feel estranged from Him at times, but God is truth and in Him is no darkness. He only desires the best for us, so let's desire that for ourselves and give Him our best. Amen!

Additional Inspiration: Psalm 30:4–5

May 24

Proverb 24:11–12
Rescue

Dear friends, we have a responsibility toward those we say we love and care about. Privacy alerts are heightened in our society, and many of us don't want to be intrusive. We want to respect others' privacy because we want the same in return. That makes sense, but only to a point. If we have friends or family who we see evidence that they are hurting themselves and others, with bad choices and habits, we have a responsibility to say something.

As a doctor, I am required to report elder and child abuse. Even a hint of suspicion is a mandate for all providers to make the call to Adult Protective Services or Child Protective Services. Hold back or rescue those who are perishing. Remember we are Yahweh's hands and feet, and we are His ambassadors. We don't have to be pushy. We only need to do our part to help our loved ones who are being led astray. Pray and be blessed!

Additional Inspiration: Psalm 34:17–18

Rx: Today be better than you were yesterday and tomorrow better than you are today. ~Dr. J

May 25

Proverb 25:12
Rebuke

An earring or an ornament of 100 percent pure gold is very expensive. If someone were to give you such an ornament as a gift, it is something most of us would go to great lengths to protect. We may place it in a special place where nothing or no one could get to it. Depending on the size, we may even choose to put it in a safe deposit box. Whatever we chose to do, it would be to maintain the value of such an expensive gift.

It is notable that Yahweh equates the rich value of such a gift to the value of receiving Godly rebuke or advice. That is powerful! We are always learning and growing, and because of this we will make mistakes, offend others and ourselves. We are not above reproach, Amen! Next time you find yourself subject to Godly correction, remember its value in gold. Selah!

Additional Inspiration: Psalm 141:5

May 26

Proverb 26:11
Folly

This is indeed an interesting factoid but nonetheless ever so disgusting in thought and action. If you have ever cared for or owned a dog, you may have witnessed this firsthand. Why the drastic comparison between dogs' vomit and human folly? As easily as it is for us to comprehend how non-sensible returning to our vomit is, we must understand that Yah sees our return to our folly just as stupid.

We will out of foolishness repeat things that hurt us and are bad for our health emotionally, physically, and emotionally. He shares this insight with us to let us understand the way of a fool. Next time you find yourself struggling with repeat folly, just imagine the dog vomit. You have the power to change the outcome. Be blessed!

Additional Inspiration: Psalm 69:5

Rx: Today be better than you were yesterday and tomorrow better than you are today. ~Dr. J

May 27

Proverb 27:8
Stray

To stray is to go off course, to not go in the intended direction. When a little bird leaves the nest too early, it may not be ready for the world at large. Combined with losing its support system, the little bird easily becomes susceptible to the dangers of the big world. Likewise, when we stray too early from our physical and/or spiritual home, we may face negative consequences.

Of course we grow up and leave our parents' home to create our own home, but what God is really warning us about is leaving the path of righteousness that He has placed us on. We must be careful to not turn to the right or left but stay the course, with our eyes fixed on Him. There are benefits and rewards that await us. Shalom!

Additional Inspiration: Psalm 40:16

May 28

Proverb 28:13
Renounce

Dear friend, this verse is a beautiful reminder of what Yeshua did for us on the cross and the reality of what Yahweh makes new to us every day. His grace and mercies for us are a daily renewable energy that we don't have to pay for. His only ask of us is that we be honest, love, and obey. Our confessions aren't for God as much as they are for us. By owning up to our nastiness and not being wise in our own eyes, God uses our transparency to heal us.

He sees our confessions as an act of humility and the posture of humbleness in our heart. The enemy wants you to be a slave to your sin, but this can be overcome by simply opening your mouth and speaking. Be bold and press on. Shalom!

Additional Inspiration: Psalm 79:8–9

Rx: Today be better than you were yesterday and tomorrow better than you are today. ~Dr. J

May 29

Proverb 29:8
Mockers

We have seen riots and protests that have taken place over the years and how violent and dangerous life can be within the heat of the moment. We serve a God of justice, Elohim. No doubt, injustice, oppression, and ignoring the voice of the needy is detestable to Him. It upsets Him and so it should us. However, we must always come in the spirit of Yah, the spirit of Christ, and the great peace leaders of our time, such as Martin Luther King, Jr., Mahatma Gandhi, Nelson Mandela, and Cesar Chavez. #PeacefulProtest. We cannot let anger lead us to move in the wrong spirit. Pray and let God use you to make life better for others while you are here. Shalom!

Additional Inspiration: Psalm 9–3, 5

May 30

Proverb 30:7-8
Desire

Desire to walk in the truth. Truth is true and it cannot lie. God rewards people who want to live the right way and who choose to live with honesty, integrity, and justice in their hearts, minds, and actions. Imagine how big God must have smiled when this prayer reached His ears. The speaker in this Proverb was asking God for a certain lifestyle, one that is set on a firm foundation of truth and aligned with Yah's kingdom. Let's all be as bold as the speaker of this Proverb and ask God to do the same for us. Pray He receive our requests before we die and to keep truth on our lips. Selah!

Additional Inspiration: Psalm 91:11-12

May 31

Proverb 31:16
Considers

Some of the decisions we have to make in this life are so tough that oftentimes we don't know what to do or who to call. No one seems to have the answers we need. Does this sound familiar? When we walk with Yah, we walk by faith. Faith in some regard is blind in that we believe in the unseen. When we have to make tough life decisions, let us remember that God wants us to always consult with and trust Him first. Look at a situation from all angles and seek wise counsel, but always be methodical and pray. Ask Jehovah! He will always guide you on a firm path. Amen!

Additional Inspiration: Psalm 102:1–2

JUNE

Whoever gives heed to instruction prospers, and blessed is he who trusts in the Lord.

Proverb 16:20

June 1

Proverb 1:15
Path

Yahweh wants what is best for us all the time. Proverbs is full of daily wisdom on how to govern ourselves and how to interact with our communities. It is a no-brainer that when we think good thoughts, it leads to right behavior, but sometimes we need a reminder. We fool ourselves when we think we can walk down wicked paths and purposely commit acts that are not healthy without consequences.

We will indeed encounter hardships and negative consequences. Even with right living, we will face trials and tribulations. The truth we hold to is that we serve a just and merciful God who promises us a hope, a future, to bless us, and not harm us. Trust and believe it!

Additional Inspiration: Psalm 62:10

June 2

Proverb 2:10
Knowledge

Ask, seek, knock, and you will receive. Yah tells us if we want wisdom, all we must do is ask. Super simple concept, right? When we are ready to grow and leave our child-like mindset behind, God is immediately on the scene, ready to present us with spiritual adult pleasantries. Most of us enjoy something pleasing to our senses, so how much more can we rejoice in feeding our soul with spiritual sweetness?

When we decide to do the adult-thing (go "adulting"), wisdom dwells in our heart. The byproduct of this indwelling is better thinking, improved decision making, and elevated living. The positive effects in turn spill over into our circles of influence. Shalom!

Additional Inspiration: Psalm 19:9–10

June 3

Proverb 3:9–10
Firstfruits

There is power in the transaction of giving. When we live our lives with an open hand rather than a closed one, we are not only in a giving position, but a receiving stance as well. It feels good to share, especially out of abundance. God loves a cheerful giver, and He promises to reward those who trust Him with their time, talent, and treasure (yes, our moolah!).

These are just three ways in which we bless Yahweh and others. Live with an open hand and give to your church and charities, donate your professional services, and volunteer. Then, watch how your life overflows with blessings from God. Tithing works!

Additional Inspiration: Psalm 1:3

June 4

Proverb 4:11–12
Stumbled

God promises to protect and guide us with His wisdom that is in our hearts. We may not understand everything at every moment, but that doesn't negate His promise or make it any less real. We don't serve a God of trickery. Of mystery yes, but trickery no. Our God wants to reveal Himself to us and have an intimate relationship with us. When we walk with God we will of course have trials and temptations, but He promises that we will remain untouched, free to walk without hampering, and free to run without stumbling. Hallelujah!

Additional Inspiration: Psalm 118:13–14

June 5

Proverb 5:12
Spurned

Danger alert! Stop and think for a moment how our world would be if children were never disciplined or corrected. Consider how many whining, kicking, screaming tantrums would be played out in the higher courts. Would we all still be in diapers because we refuse to wear the pull-ups? Although this is silly to think about, the point is that instruction, discipline, rebuke, correction, and feedback are all necessary tools for success. Parents have to do this every day for eighteen-plus years of their children's lives.

We all know that at some point, we adult kids don't want to listen to our parents; however, there's an inherent danger when we live this way. We bring unwanted trouble on ourselves and end up trying to blame others for our unfortunate circumstances. Just like an earthly parent, our spiritual parent, Jehovah, wants to protect us from unseen or seen danger.

Let's practice being open to His way of raising us. He works everything for the good of those who love Him and He disciplines those He loves, like a good parent does. Praise the most high God, Yahweh! Shalom.

Additional Inspiration: Psalm 51:1–2

Rx: Today be better than you were yesterday and tomorrow better than you are today. ~Dr. J

June 6

Proverb 6:18
Devises

Have you ever felt like someone set you up to fall? Ever felt like someone was scheming against you? Yahweh tells us in this Proverb that there are people in this world who plot and devise wicked schemes and are quick to do the wrong thing. Thankfully this behavior is detestable to Yah and He says, "Vengeance is mine."

We often get outraged about this or that injustice that has happened to us and want to take matters into her own hands. All the while, forgetting that Yah is our vindicator. Since we were made in the image of our Creator, it shouldn't come as a surprise that we have this emotion. However, it would be wise of us to remember that we serve a God of justice, and He will declare victory for those who love Him. Amen!

Additional Inspiration: Psalm 10:17–18

Rx: Today be better than you were yesterday and tomorrow better than you are today. ~Dr. J

June 7

Proverb 7:7
Judgment

We can learn a lot from the Proverbs if we ask God for wisdom and discernment. We are easily deceived when we don't have our full trust in Yahweh. When we don't ask the Holy Spirit for help, we walk in our own strength and our judgment fails. Trust that our Creator wants to protect us and bless us. Wisdom can be learned and given. God wouldn't tell us to ask for it if He was not willing to give it. That would be mean and we serve a loving God. Right? Ask God for more wisdom and continue your study of Proverbs to increase your knowledge. Be blessed!

Additional Inspiration: Psalm 143:10

June 8

Proverb 8:14
Counsel

Wisdom is one of the most valuable life tools that we can possess and master. When we put on our spiritual protectors, we really get a big bang for the buck. It's like getting a deal when you go shopping; you get more than you bargained for. When we obtain wisdom, we are in route to receive counsel, sound judgment, understanding, and ultimately power. With these features activated and in your arsenal, you can conquer any situation that you encounter. This is what it means when we say, "We can do all things through Him who gives us strength." Shalom!

Additional Inspiration: Psalm 147:5

Rx: Today be better than you were yesterday and tomorrow better than you are today. ~Dr. J

June 9

Proverb 9:9
Teach

Rejoice in the promises of the Lord! We serve a God who wants the best for us and wants to reward us in this life as well as in the life to come. Yahweh wants us to be teachable creatures so He can use us to fulfill His will through our lives. We can grow in our wisdom and add to our learning. Just like an accomplished musician or athlete, practice makes permanent. In contrast, when we are not teachable, we can't learn and we can't grow. Meditate on this today and think about areas in your life where you need to allow Yahweh to teach and transform you. Selah!

Additional Inspiration: Psalm 51:6

June 10

Proverb 10:16
Wages

Have you ever wondered why some people with good income have constant trouble with finances? Our wages represent the treasure that God has given us to steward over. How we use our money is what we sow. What we sow is what we reap. If you use your wages to tithe, pay bills, buy healthy food, and have a gym membership, you bring life and a good name upon yourself. When you don't handle your responsibilities and use your income for unhealthy food and sedentary activities, you bring harm on yourself. So go ahead tithe, save, invest, and make better choices. The abundant life is yours for the taking. Shalom!

Additional Inspiration: Psalm 44:3

June 11

Proverb 11:14
Advisors

Friends, we all agree that we not only want victory in our life, but we would like sure victory. Amen? Check it out: Yahweh promises to give a nation sure victory with good intentions, planning, guidance from many experts, and proper execution. Action undertaken without preparation may lead to success, but in many situations it simply leads to failure and/or detour.

Sometimes we suffer unnecessary consequences that can be costly in time, emotion, and finances. We can see this occurring in many levels of humanity. Take time today to be conscious of the fact that we are indeed at the mercy of not only God, but also those He has put in positions of power. Pray for the leaders of the nations of the world and all its inhabitants. Shalom!

Additional Inspiration: Psalm 46:6

Rx: Today be better than you were yesterday and tomorrow better than you are today. ~Dr. J

June 12

Proverb 12:15
Foolish

If you have ever experienced thinking you were going the right way only to find out you were lost, you know how frustrating and a little scary this can be. Being lost is usually not a fun experience for us. When we finally find our way or get help from someone who knows the right way, we experience an overwhelming sense of joy and relief. And if we remain stubborn and don't listen, we stay lost.

This Proverb describes a foolish person, who refuses to listen to advice and believes their wisdom to be supreme. Yahweh encourages us throughout Scripture to listen and consult with elders and advisers. We can't think we know it all. It behooves us to build relationships with a few God-fearing people who we can go to for advice. Selah!

Additional Inspiration: Psalm 143:8

Rx: Today be better than you were yesterday and tomorrow better than you are today. ~Dr. J

June 13

Proverb 13:11
Dishonest

Dear friends, in the fast-paced, drive-through, ready-made, at-your-service era that we live in, it is tempting to want to take the easy route to acquire more products and money. We may decide that we want something so bad that we put it on plastic and pay more for it today than it will be worth tomorrow.

Unfortunately many of us have been duped into accepting the pseudo-money or quick money model of life. Many infomercials and Internet ads bait us with the idea that following their secret method will lead us to become wealthy in a short time. In the fine print their disclosure reads "results vary," and we all know what that means. The truth is that it takes time to build anything substantial, including wealth.

Some wealthy people are financially fit because they adopted the principle of gathering and saving money over time. God promises to reward those who make good use of their time, talent, and treasure. Pray, tithe, invest, and be blessed. Amen!

Additional Inspiration: Psalm 107:37–38, 43

Rx: Today be better than you were yesterday and tomorrow better than you are today. ~Dr. J

June 14

Proverb 14:15
Simple

Any of us can be gullible at times, but let's face it, if we were always being taken advantage of or never making good choices, we would be in trouble way more often. Most of us opt for living a stable life because living a risky and dangerous life isn't safe or sustainable. Awareness is the one key to living a healthier life. It is wise to analyze our motives, thoughts, plans, and actions—especially before we involve ourselves with others and make major decisions.

Do your homework on the company before signing the contract. Read up on the organization before buying online. Research the product and read the reviews. We don't have to overanalyze, but we must do our due diligence to educate ourselves in the life choices we make. In everything always consult with God and trusted advisors. Amen!

Additional Inspiration: Psalm 16:7–8

Rx: Today be better than you were yesterday and tomorrow better than you are today. ~Dr. J

June 15

Proverb 15:14
Discerning

Yahweh makes a clear distinction between those who pursue a righteous path and those who do not. When we operate from a place of discernment, we desire the ability to see a situation or person clearly, as God sees it. This requires the action of seeking out the truth. In this way we grow in knowledge, good and bad, and are better able to give sound advice and to know the way we should go. This is the depth of relationship God wants us to aspire for and attain.

By comparison, foolish people are simply gullible, without filter, and say things that are not wise, not edifying nor inspiring. They don't look for wisdom but find more pleasure in gossiping. We must remember that God is watching us. What kind of person do you want Him to see? Selah!

Additional Inspiration: Psalm 119:35

June 16

Proverb 16:20
Trusts

Let's take heed indeed! Who doesn't want prosperity and to be blessed by God? To be prosperous means to have insight, make good decisions, and have an abundance of goodness in our life. To be blessed is to receive favor from the Lord in a variety of ways. From love, profession, health, family, finance, peace, and joy.

You name it: every good gift comes from above. The Lord of the universe and all creation, Jehovah, is a personal God, and when we stop to listen and then act on His instruction, we go in the direction He intends. When we trust Him, He gives us wings to fly. Pray and meditate on this. Invite Yahweh to help you take heed and trust. Amen!

Additional Inspiration: Psalm 37:3

June 17

Proverb 17:14
Quarrel

"Can't we all just get along?" These famous words uttered by Rodney King still ring true today. Unfortunately until our Lord Jesus Christ returns, we will encounter strife, trials, and tribulations. However, we can strive to be righteous in every encounter we have. Yahweh has given us the command to love. When we love, we ought not to argue, quarrel, or be hot-tempered. God asks us to live peaceful lives, and although this may be hard to attain at all times, it is attainable.

Arguing is a choice, and we can choose not to quarrel with one another. Yahweh understands that we may have intense discussions, but He wants us to know the limits and boundaries in this area. Arguments often lead us to say and do things we later regret. Next time you feel the urge to argue, stop, think, and take a break or walk. Reflect on this Proverb, keeping peace and love in the forefront at all times. Shalom!

Additional Inspiration: Psalm 85:10

June 18

Proverb 18:10
Name

Dear friends, we must get ourselves into the habit of calling God by His name. When we use the word "God" in our hearts, we have an idea of who we are referencing, but it is not purposely directed without using His name. Think about when someone says hello to you. Doesn't it sound a little warmer when they actually use your correct name and even more so when they add a nice adjective with it, like "sweet Betty"?

Well so it is with God. God is our Heavenly Father and some of His names are Jehovah, Adonai, El Shaddai, Ruach Elohim, Yahweh, Prince of Peace, Alpha Omega, and many more. Each name has a different meaning, purpose, and intention. Start using His many names today and experience the strong tower of God. Amen!

Additional Inspiration: Psalm 9:9–10

Rx: Today be better than you were yesterday and tomorrow better than you are today. ~Dr. J

June 19

Proverb 19:15
Laziness

Movement and staying in motion is one of the keys to life. God ordered us to have a Sabbath day after we have worked six days. Most of us should not be exempt from work, unless of course one is disabled or in retirement years. Movement yields many benefits to us mentally, spiritually, and physically. Have you ever noticed how you have more energy after you work out and less when you have laid around all day or overslept? Every able-bodied adult has the responsibility to take care of himself or herself. We cannot be a society that rewards laziness and irresponsibility, but we can be empathetic and encouraging to those down on their luck. Shalom!

Additional Inspiration: Psalm 146:9

June 20

Proverb 20:15
Rare

Dear friend, reading and studying the Proverbs is a powerful activity. When you study and meditate on any subject and begin to discuss it with others, you reach a point where you are fluent with the subject matter. So it is with studying the Proverbs. You will begin to think and speak in ways that impart wisdom. Be ready to be the oddball in some circles. As this Proverb indicates, people who speak wisely are a rarity. They are indeed hard to find.

It is much easier to find people who speak rashly, loosely, without substance, and state falsehoods with evil intent (i.e. gossips). This behavioral fact is easily observed with many of our reality TV shows. Take a little time to censor your speech. It is okay to be different. Our Creator set us apart for something better and we will be blessed. Amen!

Additional Inspiration: Psalm 12:6–8

Rx: Today be better than you were yesterday and tomorrow better than you are today. ~Dr. J

June 21

Proverb 21:17
Pleasure

Let's pray God give us wisdom to show restraint. Amen! We must be smart stewards of our time, talents, and treasures. In Western industrialized cultures, the theme is to spend, spend, spend. Why, you only live once, right? Get it now! You can have it today! Deals and steals surround us and can be easily attained with a click.

If we want to build wealth or have a savings for emergency, college, or retirement, then we must shift our thinking to a save, save, save mentality. The reality is that sometimes or most times, we just can't afford it at the moment. We must to learn to recognize the difference between our needs and our wants. Practice self-control to yield positive life-changing results. Selah!

Additional Inspiration: Psalm 119:25–56

June 22

Proverb 22:9
Blessed

This Proverb is the tenet of the sayings, "give more, get more," "you reap what you sow," and "karma, dharma." However we phrase it, this Proverb gets to the crux of the action. We have to live a life of generosity and really see it as a mandate from God. We are made in Adonai's image, and He gave fully in and of Himself literally in Jesus's death, burial, and resurrection.

We owe Him everything we have and all that we are. His word says, "When we do unto the least of these we give unto God." So, here's the challenge: stop holding back and holding out. Give generously and watch how you in turn are blessed. Shalom!

Additional Inspiration: Psalm 37:21

Rx: Today be better than you were yesterday and tomorrow better than you are today. ~Dr. J

June 23

Proverb 23:17-18
Zealous

Dear friend, it is important that we pay close attention to this Proverb. It is very easy to want to go along to get along. Why, everyone else is doing it. When we fear people, their opinions, acceptance, and rejection, it leads us to do and say things that please people and not God. Of course we must love our neighbor as ourselves and be mindful of others, but this is never at the expense of our faith and our reverence to Yah.

Don't be deceived by those who intentionally walk in sin and have no respect for God. To be zealous for the Lord means we are fired up about His ways and His purpose. When we fear Him we desire to walk right with Him, knowing that our hope and our future are sure. Let's think! Selah.

Additional Inspiration: Psalm 42:1-2

June 24

Proverb 24:13-14
Wisdom

Dear friends, if we claim to believe in Yahweh and the Scriptures, then it should follow that we believe all that is written, especially that which is written about with much frequency. Wisdom is definitely supreme in Yah's eyes, and that is not only evident in creation itself, but it is also prominent throughout the word of God. With that simple understanding, it would behoove us to pray earnestly for wisdom on a daily basis. We need the wisdom of our Creator to guide us toward the future hope that only He alone can promise to never cut off. Pray and believe. Amen!

Additional Inspiration: Psalm 119:101–103

June 25

Proverb 25:15
Gentle

Dear friend, our Creator wants us to exercise caution in the area of communication. Although we have so-called freedom of speech, it is not to be translated as freedom to say what we want, when we want, how we want. On the contrary, freedom of speech is to have the wisdom to choose and use our words wisely. Let our behavior align with our dialogue. Yahweh promises us that we catch more blessings when we exercise patience and calm speech. The Word says "a gentle tongue can break a bone," meaning people will yield. These are promises from God; try it and see. Be blessed!

Additional Inspiration: Psalm 31:23–24

June 26

Proverb 26:12
Wise

What's worse than a fool? Someone wise in his or her own eyes. According to Yahweh, the arrogant, boastful, self-absorbed person runs a greater risk of downfall than a fool. Haughty eyes and a proud heart are detestable to our God. Although we are fearfully and wonderfully made, we must not allow knowledge of that fact to lead us astray in thought and action. God has great plans for us! It's only when we follow His wisdom, not our own, that we receive the blessings He has waiting for us. Let's think!

Additional Inspiration: Psalm 69:6

Rx: Today be better than you were yesterday and tomorrow better than you are today. ~Dr. J

June 27

Proverb 27:9
Incense

The mind, body, and spirit can be satisfied through the provocation of our senses. Throughout the Scriptures, Jehovah makes references to the pleasing aroma of burning sacrifice and likens it to sweet incense. Can you see how we, made in His image, also enjoy the pleasing aromas of various things? The perfume, beauty, home care, and food industries have capitalized on this fine creative feature we bear. Pleasant smells are healing to our physical and mental selves.

Likewise, honesty and truth are healing to our spiritual senses. Think back to a time when you had a healthy conversation with a good friend. The exchange of listening, empathizing, and learning in and of itself is an example of a healthy life-giving relationship. Praise God for those in your life that you can call earnest friends. Shalom!

Additional Inspiration: Psalm 71:23–24

Rx: Today be better than you were yesterday and tomorrow better than you are today. ~Dr. J

June 28

Proverb 28:14
Fears

To always fear the Lord means that we always stand in awe of Him, revere Him, and show Him respect—much like the respect we show our parents. We may have grown up with a healthy or not so healthy fear of our parents. Out of respect and a desire to not disappoint them and to stay out of trouble with them, we knew how to walk the line. Is it not true that we preferred our parents be in a good mood when we were growing up, rather than a bad one? So it is the same with God.

When we don't give thought to our ways and show no respect for Jehovah's authority or others, our heart is hard. When we fall into the place of a hard heart, we can easily fall into trouble and face dire consequences. Yahweh always has our best interest at heart and wants to give us godly desires. Fear, love, trust, and obey Him. Shalom!

Additional Inspiration: Psalm 112:1

June 29

Proverb 29:10
Bloodthirsty

No, this isn't a case for vampires! However, if the imagery works to help us understand the power of this verse, so be it. The fact is we are in a spiritual war between light and darkness, but we already know the victor is Yahweh! As you read this verse, you can quickly see men and women, in your mind's eye, of whom this verse applies, even today.

Jesus Christ died at the hands of bloodthirsty villains such as these. Modern men of integrity such as Dr. Martin Luther King, Jr., and President John F. Kennedy were assassinated by evil men working to destroy light. There are many others who have died sacrificially. We should remember to pray for our brothers and sisters around the globe who are being persecuted for their faith and righteousness. God protect them and bless them today. Shalom!

Additional Inspiration: Psalm 34:17–18

June 30

Proverb 30:8–9
Dishonor

Sometimes we get caught up wanting more in life, but this verse reminds us to appreciate having just enough. It is definitely a positive thing for us to aspire to be better versions of ourselves and to be our best for others. Yahweh intentionally set purpose in us that manifests through the dreams and desires of our hearts.

This verse, however, is speaking to a posture of our heart. We would never want to be in a position where we steal to eat or are so rich that we think we are self-sufficient. These are dangerous postures to take on. Today, thank the God of abundance that we have just enough. Amen!

Additional Inspiration: Psalm 91:14–16

Rx: Today be better than you were yesterday and tomorrow better than you are today. ~Dr. J

JULY

Hope deferred makes the heart sick, but a longing fulfilled is a tree of life.
                              Proverb 13:12

JULY 1

Proverb 1:20
Wisdom

Wisdom poses herself for all to see. Thank God for this! If wisdom raises her voice in the public square, she is, in a sense, obvious for all to see and hear. In addition, she wants to be known and used by all. Wisdom was present before God created us and wants to be an active part of our lives. Every person in the forest benefits from a compass, whether they feel lost or not. How much more so when they know they are lost?

Wisdom through the Holy Spirit is our life compass. Meditate on these truths. Ask God to impart wisdom upon you. Call aloud to wisdom and invite her in. Listen for her speaking to you and be ready to act. Be Blessed!

Additional Inspiration: Psalm 119:68

JULY 2

Proverb 2:11
Discretion

Throughout the early Proverbs, God is calling us to do some spiritual vetting. Yah is commanding us to walk wisely because it is a safe way to maneuver through this life experience. Yahweh isn't suggesting we won't have trouble. Jesus stated: "In this world you will have trouble but lo that I have overcome the world." It is the wisdom of God that guarded and protected us from eternal spiritual death. It is the same God who desires to guard and protect us during our earthly journey through His wisdom, discretion, and understanding. Lean on Him!

Additional Inspiration: Psalm 119:125

JULY 3

Proverb 3:11–12
Discipline

Yahweh loves us and He wants us to live healthy, productive, fruitful lives. He is our spiritual father, and He has a responsibility to direct us. When we are willing to participate with Him, the experience can be a little smoother than when we choose to be antagonistic to His guidance. Do parents not discipline their children from time to time because of behavior issues? Of course they do! And so it is with our spiritual father. Many of us don't want to listen to our earthly parents as we get older, but Yah knows we still need a father. We must learn to trust Him with it all because He truly knows what is best for us. Shalom!

Additional Inspiration: Psalm 18:17–18

JULY 4

Proverb 4:13
Instruction

Can you think of one activity or piece of major equipment that doesn't come with instructions? Almost everything we do or use requires instruction. Instruction and carefully followed directions are so important that manufacturers will put wording on packages to "Read instructions first before using." Some of us choose to follow the recommendation because we honestly desire the best outcome. Others of us just go for it and don't give any thought to following instructions.

This is the "I will figure it out as I go" mentality. For some, this yields decent results, but for many, the mistakes along the way cost us too much unnecessary time and stress. Well, life is much like this example, and God has given us the B.I.B.L.E. ("Basic Instructions Before Leaving Earth") to guide and direct our steps in a place we have never been before. Keep reading, seeking, and holding the Word close to your heart. Shalom!

Additional Inspiration: Psalm 86:1–4

JULY 5

Proverb 5:13
Obey

Sound like anyone you know? Google has allowed us to believe that all knowledge is just a click away and that everything is DIY. While self-teaching is a great asset to possess, we are still at the mercy of the world around us, and ultimately there are some things we can't look up on the Internet or even read in a book. Some wisdom comes through conversation and listening to the instruction from God Himself or whomever He chooses to speak through.

Friends, let's snap out of our technological daze and get real with ourselves, others, and God. Listen to what you believe He instructs you to do. Be respectful and listen to those in a position to encourage and challenge you. Trust feedback from those you trust and don't waste time clinging to habits, ideas, thought patterns, actions, conversations, and relationships that are toxic, negative, or damaging. Listen up and take action because God wants to bless you. Amen!

Additional Inspiration: Psalm 119:129–130

Rx: Today be better than you were yesterday and tomorrow better than you are today. ~Dr. J

JULY 6

Proverb 6:19
Dissention

Do you ever feel bothered by the corruption and greed you see played out in the news? We are dismayed when these tragedies hit close to home. Whether in our workplaces, educational spaces, government high places, or within our own families, we see evil, demonic, fleshly behaviors exhibited. Although it is hard for one to admit, all humans have bias and motive.

Some are healthier biases and motives than others. When we are victims of someone's negative biases or ill motives, we experience the painful consequences. We may be tempted to question whether God loves us and cares. Please know that He does. This Proverb says our Lord detests this type of behavior. Nothing is hidden from Him, and He will have the last word. Trust and believe it. Shalom!

Additional Inspiration: Psalm 147:10–11

JULY 7

Proverb 7:10
Crafty

Dear friends, stay on guard! James states that the devil is like a roaring lion, roaming to and fro throughout the earth looking for those to devour. The enemy and cronies work in cleverly deceptive ways. Once we understand their M.O., we don't have to be surprised. Sometimes sin will be so obvious, as in this Proverb. Who could miss this woman so described? Other times it isn't so obvious but it looks good, as with those who have crafty intentions. Pray about everything before getting involved. Invite God into all the decisions you make. Hallelujah, there is protection against the enemy in the name of Yeshua!

Additional Inspiration: Psalm 119:113

JULY 8

Proverb 8:15-16
Govern

Kings, rulers, princes, nobles, queens, presidents and czars—no matter where in the world we live, we are surrounded by leadership. A few select people who make decisions that greatly affect the masses. To some degree we are at their mercy, and oftentimes in many countries people have suffered and lost their lives due to the decisions made by the elect in charge.

As hard as it may be to see in the world that appears to be in a downward spiral, Yahweh will have the final word. Although hard to understand, He allows every ruler their turn. Good and bad, He sees it all, and they will have to give an account. Trust and believe that Jehovah Jireh will bring justice. Stay in prayer!

Additional Inspiration: Psalm 2:10-11

JULY 9

Proverb 9:10
Fear

It is good for us to have a healthy fear of Yahweh. This fear is a feeling of reverence, similar to how many of us felt about our parents. Fearing our parents as children and as adults keeps us from doing or saying something without respect. The same honor we show our parents can carry over into how we treat others and ourselves and can affect the decisions we make. When we give thought to our ways, we can avoid painful mistakes and extend more love and mercy to others. Keep walking with Him!

Additional Inspiration: Psalm 119:103

JULY 10

Proverb 10:17
Heeds

When it comes to children, we understand the notion of modeling behavior. Kids may or may not say much, but they are listening and watching. Where do they learn their first curse word? Why do we act shocked? The truth is that this modeling of behavior never stops. As Christians we are called to be perfect as Christ is perfect.

We must be wise about this and realize that when we accept correction from Yahweh, it allows us to be models of Jesus on this earth. When we say we belong to Him but ignore His correction, we are teaching those who are watching and listening the wrong thing, hence leading them astray. God wants us to apply this concept of modeling behavior to everyone we are in community with. Be mindful and be blessed!

Additional Inspiration: Psalm 51:10–13

Rx: Today be better than you were yesterday and tomorrow better than you are today. ~Dr. J

JULY 11

Proverb 11:19
Attains

All throughout the Scriptures, it is obvious that we are stuck with the unique human gift of free choice. Although we have contingencies placed on us by age due to laws, at a certain point in life we become accountable to ourselves and Yahweh. This Proverb sheds light on the fact that we play a large part in the experience we realize on Earth.

We can get right spiritually, mentally, and physically and attain life, health, prosperity, peace, love, and joy. Or we can walk in evil darkness and get early, painful, sudden, death. We don't like to hear it, but we do have choice. Let's get real! Sometimes it is the choices we make that we are bothered by. Seek God in everything we do. Pray that we keep choosing the light. Shalom!

Additional Inspiration: Psalm 75:6–7

Rx: Today be better than you were yesterday and tomorrow better than you are today. ~Dr. J

JULY 12

Proverb 12:16
Prudent

If you have ever played the fool of this Proverb, you are not alone; many of us have. I am raising my hand now. Let our experience be our teacher. Each time we become more aware of our being, we learn, and then God works with us to correct our behavior. If we are truly following Christ, we must strive to seek peace at all times. This is achievable when we begin to see past those hurts, wrongs, and insults that are keeping us in emotional bondage. We must remember to forgive others as Yah forgives us. Shalom!

Additional Inspiration: Psalm 103:8

JULY 13

Proverb 13:12
Deferred

Trials and tribulations will come in this life, and there is no way around that fact. Rather than worry about that, we can focus our energy on the dreams that God has set within each and every one of our hearts and minds. The hope that dwells in us allows us to access more of the life God has for us. Hope is what allows us to press on in our existence, and without it we easily become physically, emotionally, and spiritually sick.

Life devoid of hope creates an experience of helplessness and ultimately depression, which can lead to suicidal ideation, resulting in death. It is easy to lose faith in what you hope will come to pass, but never stop longing for your dreams, my friend. When our dreams are being fulfilled, we too are being filled with life. Amen!

Additional Inspiration: Psalm 145:16

JULY 14

Proverb 14:21
Kind

Let's set the record straight about who is a neighbor and who is not. What proximity exactly allows a person to qualify as your neighbor? After reading and re-reading this verse in an attempt to understand how Yahweh is making a connection between despising your neighbor and giving and being kind to the poor, it began to make sense. It follows that God wants us to see the needy as our neighbors.

Those in need are the neighbors we are not to despise. We never know how a person ended up in their circumstances until we ask them. We can, however, positively affect their lives by showing them kindness through sharing our gifts from God. In this way everyone is blessed, including God. Amen!

Additional Inspiration: Psalm 62:9

JULY 15

Proverb 15:17
Hatred

Dear friends, as we read this Proverb, the song "Can't Buy Me Love" comes to mind. It's true that it doesn't matter how much money we have, how rich we are, or how luxurious our car. Not one of these can buy sincere love and genuine kindness. There are many rich, lonely, and angry individuals and families. God desires us to have homes full of love, forgiveness, kindness, and encouragement. We should not hate anyone, let alone our family. When we store hatred in our heart, it affects us holding the hatred the most. Our body will feel the effects in various ways, even to the point of death. Be mindful of this. Focus and be blessed!

Additional Inspiration: Psalm 133:1–3

Rx: Today be better than you were yesterday and tomorrow better than you are today. ~Dr. J

JULY 16

Proverb 16:23
Promote

The Scriptures tell us that a wise person is someone who trusts in the Lord and gives thought to their ways and speech. Someone who actually cares about how they affect others will put this Proverb to use. In the United States of America and other countries, there exist freedoms of speech. This man-made rule does not account for or make wisdom the guiding principle by which we exercise this right.

This so-called freedom of speech can actually be a form of entrapment. Our words can trap us and get us into a lot of trouble if we aren't careful. A wise person's heart, if in the right place, will guard their mouth. They will use their lips to promote positive change, encouragement, constructive criticism, acknowledgment, honor, and love. In the way of being mindful, let's think, then speak. Amen!

Additional Inspiration: Psalm 103:1–5

Rx: Today be better than you were yesterday and tomorrow better than you are today. ~Dr. J

JULY 17

Proverb 17:15
Acquitting

With all the injustice sweeping the globe, we can easily doubt or wonder: where is God? We ask ourselves and others, doesn't God see what is happening? The obvious answer is He is with us, and yes He sees. He agrees with us that sin is detestable. Stop for a minute and ask yourself what would you do if you were God. Ladies and gentlemen, we are experiencing the effects of evil on the planet and freedom of human choice. Let's all pray daily against the evil and instead of pulling further away from God, draw closer to Him. Stay prayed up!

Additional Inspiration: Psalm 9:19–20

JULY 18

Proverb 18:13
Folly

Don't talk, just listen! It is quite fascinating the number of Proverbs that focus on mouth control. Being quiet, talking less, guarding our speech, and holding our tongues are recurrent recommendations. There is no doubt that communication is a big deal to God. What we say and when we say it are extremely important. In order to know how to appropriately respond, one must listen first.

Ever have someone try to complete your sentence to finish your story? Annoying, right? After they waste their breath guessing wrong, you still have to explain and perhaps re-explain the story. This is such an inefficient form of communication. So much time is wasted when rushing to speak before listening. Practice listening more today—you will be amazed at what you learn by observing rather than being the star of the show. Amen!

Additional Inspiration: Psalm 81:11–12

JULY 19

Proverb 19:16
Obey

Dear friends, we serve a God who wants us to have life and have life abundantly. Jehovah is not the author of sickness, strife, angst, poverty and injustice, criminal activity, emotional instability, and hate. These are experiences that can be brought on by our own doing or we can be born into. It is possible also for Satan himself to attack us. Yes, we will experience trials, but remember, God works everything together for the good of those who love Him.

One way we can protect ourselves from excess perilous conditions is by obeying instruction. Yahweh says when we do that we guard our life. It is when we think we know it all that we find ourselves in trouble mentally, physically, and spiritually. Be mindful, humble, and stay blessed!

Additional Inspiration: Psalm 28:7

Rx: Today be better than you were yesterday and tomorrow better than you are today. ~Dr. J

JULY 20

Proverb 20:18
Advice

Dear friends, it is "all good" to get advice before making major decisions. God wants us to! The caveat is to discern from whom you take advice and to weigh heavily their guidance. Your first line of consult should be with God, followed by other people who have relationship with God as well, who can pray to God on your behalf. Don't make major moves and only consult with yourself, because you can't know and think of everything. Yah will speak to you through people and situations. Getting guidance is a good thing, and you will benefit from it. Pray and ask God to send the right to counsel your way. Shalom!

Additional Inspiration: Psalm 144:1–2

JULY 21

Proverb 21:20
Foolish

We have all heard the saying to "save for a rainy day." Well, that is exactly what this Proverb calls us to do. Too often many of us find ourselves between a rock and a hard place because of poor life choices. Spending more than we earn or can afford, eating when we are full, or not doing the good things for ourselves or for others that we are called to do. Yes, that includes working out! Our Creator has given us a sound mind and intelligence. Pray and ask for guidance when you are unsure. Let's all get in the habit of saving for an emergency. Remember you don't have to eat it all or spend it all at once. Be wise and be blessed. Shalom!

Additional Inspiration: Psalm 199:66–67

JULY 22

Proverb 22:16
Oppresses

Although it may appear to look like those who take shortcuts, crooked paths, back alleys, and advantage of innocent people are ahead in this life, they are not. Those who lie, cheat, steal, destroy, and divide may experience transient earthly gain but not spiritual abundance. When these realms collide, we see divine intervention, and Jehovah serves long-awaited or swift justice.

In Proverb 22, Yahweh tells of His disgust for exploitation of the poor and taking advantage of the needy in court. He promises to plunder those who treat innocent people unjustly. The world may try to tell us something different, but we must try to never doubt God's love for us. Many men may make life hard for some, but ultimately Yah's word will come to pass and justice will prevail. Selah!

Additional Inspiration: Psalm 73:16–19

Rx: Today be better than you were yesterday and tomorrow better than you are today. ~Dr. J

JULY 23

Proverb 23:19
Wise

We are always like children before our Heavenly Father. He will always guide us and teach us. The world also offers an array of educators and teachers for us to learn from. While many are indeed knowledge masters with good intentions and credibility, many don't rest on the principles of Yahweh and thus lead others astray. We must train ourselves mentally, spiritually, and physically to stay on course. Don't get tired of choosing and doing the right thing. This is wisdom in action, and Abba promises to reward the wise. Friends, let's get our blessings. Amen!

Additional Inspiration: Psalm 23:19

JULY 24

Proverb 24:16
Righteous

Don't you love the stories of those rising from the ashes of tragedy to the beauty of triumph? This storyline is played out in many of our box office hits and reflects what happens in many of our lives. We are fooling ourselves if we think we will live a problem-free life. If we don't realize that at times we will fall, we may be taken by surprise when something "bad" happens and perhaps think that the world is against us.

The truth is we all will have trouble in this world because the ruler of the air is Satan himself. Praise God that our faith walk with Him allows us to remain untouched by turmoil, to rise up from it, and to win over and over again! Thank Yahweh for His mercy, grace, and provision. Wishing you peace today and always.

Additional Inspiration: Psalm 119:25–26

JULY 25

Proverb 25:18
False

A club, sword, and sharpener all share the ability to cause severe damage to the person or thing it contacts. Each of these could penetrate, debilitate, and mutilate a person. Obviously these are dangerous weapons, so we should pay attention if God compares these weapons to a person giving a false testimony. The damages are beyond severe.

There are many people in jail because of false accusations. People have lost their jobs, marriages, family, friends, and livelihood due to the evil of falsehood. Sometimes you lose your sanity in the process of trying to prove your innocence. Honesty is the best policy. It sounds cliché, but it will keep trouble at bay. Be wise and don't disguise through lies. Shalom!

Additional Inspiration: Psalm 34:13–14

JULY 26

Proverb 26:14
Hinges

King Solomon wrote with such creative realistic imagery. Thank God for this, because sometimes we just need to "dumb it down" in order to understand. One takeaway from many Proverbs is Yahweh's distaste for laziness. There are plenty of scriptures that teach us to work hard, stay busy, avoid idleness, and not sleep too much. Someone who is unwilling to work will not see much fruit in his or her life. God makes it clear that we reap what we sow, and diligent hands bring wealth. The first step every day, including weekends, is getting out of bed. Wise up and Rise up!

Additional Inspiration: Psalm 51:9–10

Rx: Today be better than you were yesterday and tomorrow better than you are today. ~Dr. J

JULY 27

Proverb 27:12
Prudent

Sometimes seeking the thrill is just not worth it. Yahweh wants us to live peaceful lives, full of health, purpose, and passion. He is not the author of chaos and confusion. God doesn't set us up for dangerous situations or to purposely make us stumble. He actually promises to make our path straight if we live righteous lives and follow Him.

Wisdom tells us to yield or stop when we see or sense the alert. When we act out of our flesh and/or without wisdom, we end up making foolish decisions that can result in suffering, not only for us, but also for those around us. It doesn't take a rocket scientist to know what is good or bad for you. Most of the time it is really our choice and ours alone. Pray, listen, wait, watch, repeat. Shalom!

Additional Inspiration: Psalm 55:22

JULY 28

Proverb 28:18
Suddenly

Dear friend, do you notice a theme in Proverb 28? We reap what we sow, folks! There is no way around this spiritual law. It is so easy to become cynical when we see the tragedies and disparities in the world around us. All too often we see the dark side winning, and some of us have come to accept it is just the way it is. But…God!

We must remember and remind ourselves daily that Yahweh is in control. One day He will return with a trumpet blast, and suddenly things will be different. Hold onto your faith, and don't let the enemy make you doubt the powerful God you serve. Why, he, Lucifer, certainly doesn't doubt Him! Even the demons tremble in fear of Jesus. Walk right, pray, and rest in the safety of His wings. Shalom!

Additional Inspiration: Psalm 7:8–9

JULY 29

Proverb 29:11
Wise

Control your soul, my friend. This is much easier said than done, but it is something we must all continue to do daily. It is very important to learn when to take time out for a break or just to cool off. It is unwise to just explode, let the lid come off, and give someone a piece of your mind. Even worse is when it's two fools giving full vent to their anger together. Talk about a psychologically, emotionally, and in some cases physically dangerous situation.

As you read Proverbs 29 more and more, you will see Yahweh warning us often about staying cool. It's cool, be cool, and not hot to get heated! Be self-controlled and stay alert. The enemy is looking and waiting for an opportunity to get you upset. Don't lose your cool! Shalom.

Additional Inspiration: Psalm 104:33–34

JULY 30

Proverb 30:11-12
Pure

Dear friends, we are living in times such as these illustrated in this Proverb. No doubt any news channel you turn to or newspaper you read will report on numerous cases of this peril. We live in a turned up and turned out society. We shouldn't be shocked when we see atrocities and hear of hypocrisies. This is the human way under flesh and demonic influence. When we choose Yah's way, we show love and mercy.

We demonstrate that we understand truth by first removing the plank from our own eye before judging another. We must be careful when we walk in arrogance and think we are without fault or sin. Only Jesus is perfect, but we strive daily to live as He lived. Stay prayed up and blessed!

Additional Inspiration: Psalm 51:17

Rx: Today be better than you were yesterday and tomorrow better than you are today. ~Dr. J

JULY 31

Proverb 31:18
Profitable

When you read the entire Proverb 31, you see that the woman described is a hustler and a grinder. She is a hard-working first-class businesswoman. She slays before the sun comes up and well until after it has gone down. Read Verses 15 and 18. She is a part of a team, taking care of her family, employees, clients, and community. She sets an example for how both men and women should conduct themselves.

Let's practice adopting some of these qualities if we haven't already. Pray for areas where you need help, and thank Yahweh for areas where you are currently excelling. It's never too late to make a profit! Be blessed!

Additional Inspiration: Psalm 23:5–6

AUGUST

Pleasant words are a honeycomb, sweet to the soul and healing to the bones.
Proverb 16:24

August 1

Proverb 1:22
Fool

The simple, the fools, and the mockers! Lord, help us to not be this way. The Proverbs do not speak of people in these categories in good light. When we yield to the universal law of reaping what we sow, the life of one who delights in mockery and hates knowledge will inevitably eat of that fruit. Perhaps you have fallen into one of these boxes and your life isn't where it should be. Don't be afraid to confess this to God.

Repent of this mindset and ask God to fill you with His ways and His thoughts. Pray directly to wisdom and understanding. We are all learning and growing. Be patient with yourself and with others, but don't stop pushing forward toward Christ like transformation. Shalom abounding!

Additional Inspiration: Psalm 1:1

August 2

Proverb 2:12
Perverse

In a society where good and bad coexist, we definitely need some form of protection. Many of us have felt the sting of being taken advantage of. Not only is it humiliating, but it can also lead to feelings of distrust toward others. These experiences and encounters have a way of dictating how we continue to approach people and situations as we move forward in life.

The truth is, we limit ourselves and our good works when we lack a support system and don't trust people. It doesn't have to be a large number, but we do need an accountability team. Pray God surround you with people with good intentions and like mind. Pray Jehovah protect you from people like those described in this Proverb. Lastly, pray He give you wisdom to discern between the two. God bless you, friend!

Additional Inspiration: Psalm 141:9–10

Rx: Today be better than you were yesterday and tomorrow better than you are today. ~Dr. J

August 3

Proverb 3:17-18
Pleasant

Got wisdom? Dear friend, if we want to live a peace-filled, pleasant life of purpose and passion, we must attain wisdom and understanding. This wisdom we seek, however, is not worldly in nature, but rather it is spiritual. We attain the wisdom of El Shaddai through prayer, reading, discussing, and meditating. God is not trying to hide from us! It is quite the contrary. He is waving at us and many times we just don't see.

Yahweh wants to lavish us with wisdom and understanding. Didn't God use wisdom to lay the foundations of the earth? Indeed! And as such, we too shall walk in the ways and paths of wisdom. Embrace life and be blessed. Amen!

Additional Inspiration: Psalm 90:14

August 4

Proverb 4:14–15
Wicked

Go on your own way! This is a command from Yahweh. He promises a unique path carved out just for you and me. In these two verses, He raises all the red flags and pleads with us to avoid evil and evil people at any and all costs. Why would God need to teach us something that seems so obvious? Simply put, our flesh.

Our sin inclination tempts us toward wrong choices, and we must be aware of this. Be attentive of the company you keep. Bad company corrupts good character and all the consequences that come with that life you will experience. Since we have a choice, choose right, choose wise, and choose life. Amen!

Additional Inspiration: Psalm 97:10

August 5

Proverb 5:14
Brink

Dear friend, bad choices lead to bad consequences as surely as 2 + 2 = 4. Even worse is when everything comes crashing down on you in full view for everyone to see. Embarrassment, shame, and perhaps even a costly fine deter many of us from going down that road again, while others of us choose to repeat our folly. If we want to be effective in our walk with God, we must constantly pay close attention to what we say, think, and feel because all of these guide what we ultimately choose to do.

Let's choose to walk in the path God has for us. We may stumble, and…get up, dust your shoulder off, confess, and continue to press. My friend, that is the kind of active faith that makes our God smile. Shalom!

Additional Inspiration: Psalm 145:14

Rx: Today be better than you were yesterday and tomorrow better than you are today. ~Dr. J

August 6

Proverb 6:20–21
Bind

In this Proverb Yah instructs us keep, do not forsake, bind, and to fasten His teaching and commands. When we imagine this in the literal sense, this is in essence the word becoming flesh within us. When an athlete goes pro, there are rules and codes of conduct, ethics, and commands that must be obeyed. During a game, there are refs to ensure the rules are being followed. The Holy Spirit is our invisible ref. We must be sensitive to the promptings and instruction, because after all, we want to play in the game, right? Let's minimize injuries by putting this into practice. Amen!

Additional Inspiration: Psalm 119:19–20

Rx: Today be better than you were yesterday and tomorrow better than you are today. ~Dr. J

August 7

Proverb 7:21
Persuasive

This is the very art of temptation, a tool for Satan, and a stumbling block to our flesh. In fact, these are the tools that many of us interact with daily. We are bombarded with media, sales, and advertising, trying to persuade us to buy a product or service. Much of the world is in the business of seduction, wanting us to be led astray. But Yah warns us that those who love the world are led astray by it and are at enmity with God. We must lose our fake lives to the world in order to gain true life. Practice saying no to those things that are not good for us. Run away from temptation, and as you resist the devil, he will flee. Press On!

Additional Inspiration: Psalm 28:3

August 8

Proverb 8:17–18
Seek

Isn't it refreshing to know that Yahweh is not hiding wisdom from us? How exactly do we go about obtaining this famous wisdom? We must seek. Seeking is the action by which we consciously and actively look for something. The awesome news is that wisdom wants to be found. Wisdom wants to engage us. Wisdom wants to love us. All the more when we find wisdom and develop a relationship with her, we will also gain riches, honor, wealth, and prosperity. I don't know about you, but that sounds like a deal to me. Today, focus on seeking and drawing near to Him. Shalom!

Additional Inspiration: Psalm 119:58

August 9

Proverb 9:11
Added

I had the privilege of knowing my great grandmother for more than thirty years. She lived 104 years! How often do we hear a senior citizen say, "If only I had more time" or "I wish I had more time"? We are consumed as a society with ways to extend life, delay aging, and remain youthful. As we get older we usually get wiser, but we don't have to wait until then to tap into wisdom. The key to living a long life is revealed here by Yahweh. The trick is just to learn this earlier rather than later. El Shaddai promises many days and years to be added to our life through wisdom. Let's go get it, shall we? Shalom!

Additional Inspiration: Psalm 25:7

August 10

Proverb 10:19
Sin

Think back to a time when you had a heated argument or discussion with someone. Maybe it was a partner, child, family, friend, coworker, or perhaps a stranger. Perhaps you or the other person had a moment when something was said that left you or the other person feeling really bad. On either end of this situation, we can learn a great deal from this Proverb. When we talk too much or don't use healing language, we have an easier time offending people. Sometimes we can have such loose and coarse conversations that we become desensitized and unaware until someone's feelings are hurt.

Practice awareness of what you speak. Be mindful to not blurt out everything that comes to mind. Hold your tongue! You will thank yourself later when you walk away from the conversation in peace knowing you have not offended anyone. Selah!

Additional Inspiration: Psalm 141:3

Rx: Today be better than you were yesterday and tomorrow better than you are today. ~Dr. J

August 11

Proverb 11:22
Discretion

True, some may view the image of a pig with a pierced nose as cute. However, the two just don't fit. Like, at all! First question is, where did the pig get the gold ring? Second question, how did the pig's nose get pierced? As incredible as the thought is, that is how Jah feels about women without discretion. And while we may not want to judge because we live in a time when we must be sensitive to everyone's freedoms, we must inject standards in our life. There are certain behaviors, attitudes, and attire that women and men must monitor in their relationship with God. Yeshua says, "Be holy because I your God am Holy." Shalom!

Additional Inspiration: Psalm 25:9

August 12

Proverb 12:18
Healing

"Sticks and stones may break my bones but words will never hurt me." How this saying became popular is a wonder, because bad words do hurt. They leave emotional scars that oftentimes are very hard to heal. Unlike a physical assault that may happen once, words get repeated and scenarios replayed in the theater of our minds, continuing the damage days, weeks, and years after the initial event. If harmful words can pierce like a sword, they can hurt you! It is not surprising then that the opposite can result in a healthier outcome.

When we speak positive words into one another and into ourselves, we actually have the power to heal our minds, bodies, and spirits. As we move through this day, let's practice being aware of our words and intentionally speaking life and love over one another and our self. In the name of Yeshua, Amen!

Additional Inspiration: Psalm 78:36–38

Rx: Today be better than you were yesterday and tomorrow better than you are today. ~Dr. J

August 13

Proverb 13:16
Prudent

The way we behave is a reflection of our thoughts and way of thinking. When we approach life, people, and situations with wisdom and understanding, we act with more patience, forgiveness, and peace. When we are easily irritated or confrontational, we expose our foolishness. This leads to awkward and embarrassing moments that can ruin relationships. We have an example of how to conduct ourselves in Yeshua. He is our role model, and following His way will lead us on the path of enlightenment. We are to be blessed, not stressed. Amen!

Additional Inspiration: Psalm 59:9

August 14

Proverb 14:23
Work

The Word teaches us that if man will not work, man shall not eat. Our God is a God of creativity and variety and has given us a plethora of jobs to choose from. There is something for everyone. Yahweh didn't say only those with doctorate degrees or those working for large corporations or those who hold government jobs will succeed. No! He said all hard work leads to profit. Even volunteer work. But mere talk will prove true and get you nowhere.

Mere talk will leave your with nothing to eat, no shelter, and no opportunity. Consider it as we do our faith. Faith without works is dead, right? So it is with our work. Without it can lead to death. We never wish poverty upon anyone. So let's get to work and inspire others to do the same. Be blessed!

Additional Inspiration: Psalm 25:12–13

Rx: Today be better than you were yesterday and tomorrow better than you are today. ~Dr. J

August 15

Proverb 15:21
Understanding

Sometimes we are the reason for something not being right in our lives, and we have to be brave and mature enough to admit it. This Proverb compares a person who actually enjoys (delights) their stupidity (lack of judgment) to a person who pursues understanding. The latter mindset leads to a straight path and a clear vision.

We all face trouble and obstacles, but God gives us a plan to get through them. When we delight in folly and are not corrected by the negative consequences we endure, we live a fruitless life. Meditate on this today. Pray for self, friends, and family who are in this way. Ask God to be a guide to the choices that are in line with His will for our lives. Be blessed!

Additional Inspiration: Psalm 37:23–24

August 16

Proverb 16:24
Healing

If you take this Proverb literally, Yahweh is telling us that our words have the power to bring life to ourselves and to others. When we use words that are uplifting and refreshing in our dialogue with one another, we really have an opportunity to initiate positive change in each other's lives. Not only do pleasant words heal our body, but they also mend and feed our soul.

Yahweh is spirit and used spoken word to create. We then, being spiritual creatures made in Yahweh's image, have the ability to speak life and death over ourselves and others. We are given the freedom to choose, so let's use words that heal. Shalom!

Additional Inspiration: Psalm 18:30

Rx: Today be better than you were yesterday and tomorrow better than you are today. ~Dr. J

August 17

Proverb 17:16
Fool

Have you ever had money and spent it on something only to later regret that you spent the money on that item or event? This is why the lotto allows you to choose between lump sum or yearly pay out! This is also why children left with trust funds are often not allowed access until they are of adult age. No matter how young or old, we can be foolish when it comes to money.

If you want to be better with money and have more of it, then start asking God for wisdom and knowledge in this area. Get on a budget and seek help from a financial professional if necessary. It's never too late to be a better steward of your God-given resources. P.S. Tithing works! Be blessed!

Additional Inspiration: Psalm 49:20

August 18

Proverb 18:14
Sustains

The health of our spirit plays a vital role in our total life experience. Yahweh shows us in this Proverb that with a healthy spirit we can endure physical sickness. Have you ever seen someone who, although sick in the hospital, perhaps in a cast or undergoing chemo, is still high in spirits? Usually we say something like, "I don't know how they are so strong and in good spirits." Dear friend, this is the space where our heavenly Father works out for the good of those who love Him. This is the sweet spot where God crushes our spirit of defeat and allows us to walk in heavenly confidence that sustains us. Shalom!

Additional Inspiration: Psalm 54:2, 4

Rx: Today be better than you were yesterday and tomorrow better than you are today. ~Dr. J

August 19

Proverb 19:17
Kind

There is everything good about being a kind person. It is a quality that will bring beauty into our life. Yahweh asks us to pay particular attention to a group of people, the poor. When we give to the needy and show them love and kindness, it is as if we are doing that very act directly unto the Lord. It is so easy for us to give to those we know: family, friends, coworkers. And some of the time these are the people who already have their needs met, and we are simply giving out of abundance in kindness. This is awesome but let's consider how we can be more effective in our giving, realizing that our gift can be life-changing for those we don't know and who are less fortunate. Give and stay blessed!

Additional Inspiration: Psalm 146:7–8

Rx: Today be better than you were yesterday and tomorrow better than you are today. ~Dr. J

August 20

Proverb 20:19
Betrays

Yahweh instructs us to avoid someone who gossips and talks too much. Avoiding people can be hard to do, especially if you work or live with someone who fits this description. Two different approaches can be taken when the gossiper is close—a family member, friend, or coworker—versus an acquaintance. If the person is an acquaintance, it's much easier to adhere to this Proverb. If it is someone closer to you, it may require simply spending less intimate time on the phone or in person. Bad company can corrupt good character, and God gives us this advice to protect us from negative consequences. Trust, pray, and follow His lead. Shalom!

Additional Inspiration: Psalm 12:1–2

August 21

Proverb 21:21
Pursue

This is the ultimate guarantee: life, prosperity, and honor. Wow! Jehovah Jireh promises this triple play of blessings when we choose and pursue love and righteousness. We are not pre-programmed robots, and we always have a choice. Even when wronged by others, which happens daily, we should still practice love and righteousness toward them. It's hard, but the word says if we pay someone with evil, evil will never leave our house. Let God be your avenger. I know it hurts and can be painful in the midst of trying circumstances, but with everything in us, we have to trust and believe God's promises never fail. Amen!

Additional Inspiration: Psalm 92:12–14

August 22

Proverb 22:17
Apply

Because we have been fearlessly and wonderfully made and have Google at our fingertips, we may be inclined to think, "We got this!" The arrogance of man rises like incense to the Lord and displeases Him. Jehovah Jireh has called us to be righteous and to depend on Him. Yes, we will still make mistakes, but it is the process of transformation that is important. To live wise in the way of prosperity and hope requires intentional action on our part.

We must desire to live peace-filled lives, not lives of turmoil and strife. So how do we do it? Jah tells us first to pay attention. This means increasing our awareness and direction of mind. Second, we must listen to His teaching and instruction. We do this by prayer, meditation, reading, listening to sermons, and engaging in fellowship with other believers. Third, He has called us to apply what we learn. Simply put, just do it. Shalom!

Additional Inspiration: Psalm 119:15–16

Rx: Today be better than you were yesterday and tomorrow better than you are today. ~Dr. J

August 23

Proverb 23:20-21
Glutton

The things that slow us down! It's interesting that God compares alcohol and food, two of the most frequent consumptions in our society, to show us where we must watch out for destruction. Just reflect on the number of restaurants that are springing up, hit food shows, various restaurant weeks, large portions, complex mixed drinks, and craft beer with high alcohol contents, and it is pretty easy to see how our Western culture fits this Proverb.

It is definitely not to say that we shouldn't enjoy life and eat and drink, but it is to say that overindulgence is a sin that comes with consequences. The top of the list is poor physical and mental health, loss of healthy relationships, and eventually an empty bank account. Open your eyes, pray, and make wise choices. Shalom!

Additional Inspiration: Psalm 68:19-20

August 24

Proverb 24:17-18
Rejoice

From the way this Proverb reads, it sounds like God take sides. Thankfully He does! We serve a God who is the God of justice and equal scales. He is the one who made the justice system, and we are the ones to pervert it. As good as it may feel to see justice get served for the guilty, we must still show a certain level of respect. We never want to lord it over the offender. We may thank God in private for redeeming us, but God warns us not to do this publicly and to evaluate the condition of our own heart.

We, as Christians, should feel some empathy for enemies. Some do corrupt things because they too are suffering as humans in a fallen world. However, if you do the crime, you also have to pay the fine and/or the time. That is justice! By rejoicing in our heart at the downfall of another, we simply engage in the spiritual repayment of evil with evil. This is not how we should walk. Let's think. Selah!

Additional Inspiration: Psalm 18:39–41

Rx: Today be better than you were yesterday and tomorrow better than you are today. ~Dr. J

August 25

Proverb 25:19
Lame

As a dentist, I know this too well! A lame tooth is definitely undependable. It cannot be trusted to do what it is designed to do because it is sick with decay. Sometimes you do treatment and remove the decay and restore the tooth back to its full function. When we are unfaithful, we are unreliable and can't be trusted to function as designed. When we allow God to take over our lives, Yeshua lives within us and restores us through the process of faithful transformation. We have the choice to walk in the fullness of who we are called to be, which is anything but lame. Be blessed!

Additional Inspiration: Psalm 27:1

August 26

Proverb 26:15
Lazy

Proverb 26 is full of wisdom regarding productivity and laziness. While it may seem hard to keep age-old habits in an ever-changing society, we must stay cognizant of our efforts. In industrialized countries where technology is being exploited to its potential, we create an ease to our lives that previous generations did not know. Yet, we should still maintain a good habit of self-care. A person unwilling to put food into their mouth and chew it is the epitome of laziness. We are the only ones who can monitor ourselves in this department. If we aren't willing to work hard, is it fair for us to expect amazing things to happen in our lives? Honesty + Action = Transformation. Shalom!

Additional Inspiration: Psalm 51:3–4

Rx: Today be better than you were yesterday and tomorrow better than you are today. ~Dr. J

August 27

Proverb 27:17
Relationships

God made us for relationships, with Him and with one another. Yahweh instructs us to be cautious of whom we befriend and to surround ourselves with upright company. Peer pressure and influence are not just a pre-teen/teenage concept. We are easily influenced and pick up bad habits at any age. God knows this and wants us to be influenced by the right people and causes.

As iron sharpens iron, we too can make profound impact with the people we interact with every day. Remember this going forward. We sharpen one another through love, serving, education, kind rebuke, an apt reply, encouragement, studying together, and praying for one another. Praise Jah for His design.

Additional Inspiration: Psalm 66:16–17

Rx: Today be better than you were yesterday and tomorrow better than you are today. ~Dr. J

August 28

Proverb 28:19
Abundant

Many of us subscribe to the notions, "work hard, play harder" and "go hard or go home." Some of us feel overworked and undervalued, but we know that not working is never an option. Hard work brings profit, reward, provisions, opportunity, experience, and purpose. This in essence is abundance!

When we decide to not work and be idle with our time or have misdirected energy and don't apply ourselves, the results are the opposite. We don't experience the abundant blessings that are promised to us. Yahweh is encouraging us to be hard workers and to be good stewards of our divine talents. Pray and choose wisely how to use your time, talent, and treasure. Selah!

Additional Inspiration: Psalm 5:12

August 29

Proverb 29:13
Oppressor

Dear friends, nothing is hidden from the eyes of The Lord. Praise God even more that He also gave us eyes to see and a mind to think. When you feel like the world is going crazy and the thought enters your brain, "Doesn't our leadership *see* what is going on?" The answer you should hear echo back is "Yes." We all see what is going on from our unique vantage points, through our own lens and according to our own agenda.

We unfortunately live in a time where right is wrong and wrong is right. Everyone knows and can see. We must do our parts to be peacemakers, love spreaders, and justice protectors. Help those who need it and keep praying. God will reward the faithful in heart. Shalom!

Additional Inspiration: Psalm 91:8–10

Rx: Today be better than you were yesterday and tomorrow better than you are today. ~Dr. J

August 30

Proverb 30:13–15
Haughty

Dear Friends, when we take a macroscopic view of the world, it is very easy to see that chaos is happening everywhere and at any given time. Do you ever wonder about this? Have you ever questioned why would God allow such chaos? This verse speaks to what has been and will be on earth—that is, humans with evil intentions and power.

Read these verses and meditate on what Yah is saying. Does it remind you of ethnic cleansing by various means? How about population control? There are people at all socioeconomic levels who have ascribed to a life of serving darkness. The word says we fight against spirits and principalities. Yet the power of the unseen God is within those who believe. So don't be afraid—be aware. Pray and help those in need. Amen!

Additional Inspiration: Psalm 113:7–9

Rx: Today be better than you were yesterday and tomorrow better than you are today. ~Dr. J

August 31

Proverb 31:20
Extends

Some of us naturally feel the call to help those less fortunate. Others of us turn a blind eye, while others have to be asked to help out or lend a hand. According to the Scriptures, we are all called to be humanitarians. This isn't a calling for the select few, the elect, or the chosen. We are all called to serve, especially to those in need. There are so many people who could use help in various ways that there is always work to be done. No one can say "I didn't know how to help" or "I don't have anything to give."

Consider making giving a lifestyle. We all possess time, talents, and treasure that we can share. You will change another human being's life. God will smile and you will be blessed. Shalom!

Additional Inspiration: Psalm 41:1–2

SEPTEMBER

The blessing of the Lord brings wealth,
and he adds no trouble to it.

Proverb 10:22

September 1

Proverb 1:23
Rebuke

Proverb 1 is full of wisdom coming out to us, pleading with us to listen and befriend her. Wisdom wants to be a part of our lives in every way. It may feel strange to think of wisdom as an entity in and of itself, but according to the Scriptures, she was from the beginning and is with God. In Proverb 1:23, wisdom shows us that we can be very hardheaded and non-teachable. When we choose not to respond to wise advice or to not take heed when danger presents, we fall into trouble, and undesired consequences soon follow.

We are considered wise when we look internally and see the error of our own way and take responsibility. Caution: Don't blame God in situations where He asked wisdom to show us right from wrong and we ignored it. According to the Scriptures, if we ask wisdom, she will make herself known to us. All we have to do is trust, ask God, and then do what He says. Amen!

Additional Inspiration: Psalm 141:5

September 2

Proverb 2:16
Wayward

As you read this Proverb, consider that adultery encompasses not only an extra-marital affair outside a covenant between two people, but it also represents our affair with the world outside our covenant relationship with Yahweh. Our Creator has asked us to conduct our lives in certain ways that preserve our mind, body, and spirit. He wants to protect us against the pro-aging cancerous ways of the world.

When we ascribe to the worldly philosophies and ways of living, acting, and speaking, we cheat on God. It is no secret, Jehovah is jealous for us because He is in love with us. Let's show Him daily how much we are in love with Him, too. Shalom!

Additional Inspiration: Psalm 17:14

Rx: Today be better than you were yesterday and tomorrow better than you are today. ~Dr. J

September 3

Proverb 3:21
Preserve

Something preserved is something kept in a state that can be saved for use at a future appointed time. We easily think of jam preserves or preserving food through canning, or land preservation. Yahweh instructs us that in the same way, spiritual preservation benefits us physically and emotionally. When we use sound judgment and discernment, we will make healthier life decisions that yield better outcomes. The word says you will know a tree by the fruit it bears. Let's honor these principles in our lives and never let them out of our sight. Our fruit will be the proof of His word preserved within our heart and mind. Shalom!

Additional Inspiration: Psalm 119:97–98

September 4

Proverb 4:20–22
Listen

We attend to what we choose and we listen to what we want. This is truth. It is also true that what we attend to and listen to either brings us down, keeps us where we are, or brings us up to a new level of glory. It is important that we understand how this simple concept determines much of our life experience. It's so easy to follow the pattern and pulse of the world. Whether this culture, that sector or clique, we make a choice as to who or what we follow.

If we follow Christ, we must pay close attention to the written word of God and the spoken word He whispers to our hearts. The only way to keep someone or something in your heart is to have an active relationship. Friends, let's keep our focus on daily prayer and fellowship with our Abba/Father. Shalom!

Additional Inspiration: Psalm 19:8

Rx: Today be better than you were yesterday and tomorrow better than you are today. ~Dr. J

September 5

Proverb 5:20
Captivated

According to the American Psychological Association, 20 percent to 40 percent of marriages end due to infidelity, a topic the Lord brings up a lot in His word, and obviously for good reason. Marriage is a covenant union between two people becoming one. It is to be honored and never disrespected. Likewise, the church is the bride, and we are in union with Jesus Christ. We are in a covenant with Him, a relationship set apart. We must continually self-examine and remove anything that is in the way of our relationship with Yeshua. Repent and keep your eyes fixed on Yahweh. Shalom!

Additional Inspiration: Psalm 141:8

September 6

Proverb 6:22
Guide

If only we had a crystal ball to show us our future. Have you ever known someone who has consulted a medium? Many of us have seen it depicted in the movies where the medium looks into the crystal ball and gives the seeker wisdom and advice. Well, let's give praise and thanks to Jehovah that we don't have to go that route. We have something much better than a glass full of water.

God does not want to hide our future from us. He wants quite the opposite. He desires greatly to show us more than we could have imagined; however, we must do our part in seeking Him out, reading the Scriptures, and putting what we learn into practice. Then, listen for the still, small voice. He will tell you the way to go. Amen!

Additional Inspiration: Psalm 32:8–9

Rx: Today be better than you were yesterday and tomorrow better than you are today. ~Dr. J

September 7

Proverb 7:23
Cost

Let's keep it real! We can be naïve, even as adults. Some things look, taste, feel, smell, and sound so good that we just have to have it. Maybe someone's beauty intrigues your eye, or a triple-layered chocolate cake drizzled with the creamiest frosting. It may be the alluring sound of new gossip or the smell of your married co-worker's cologne that you feel you just can't resist. Yah tells us too much of the world is not good for us. When we pursue the temptations of the world, we become ensnared, and it can cost us our life. Let's meditate on where we can improve in our lives. Be blessed!

Additional Inspiration: Psalm 135:15–18

September 8

Proverb 8:22-23
Appointed

The idea of wisdom itself being an active part of creation is a mind-elevating thought. It only makes sense that God has wisdom. But when we read that wisdom herself was appointed by the Creator, it makes it more official that we serve a God of details. God has an appointment for everything in His creation, including you and me. Nothing done by Yahweh is accidental. Amen!

Additional Inspiration: Psalm 136:5

September 9

Proverb 9:12
Wisdom

Many of us have heard the psychology terms "positive reinforcement" and "negative reinforcement." The idea that behavior or action can be encouraged and built in either a good or bad direction should cause us to take heed. In Proverbs 9:12, Yahweh describes the scenario. Wisdom will always reinforce good choices and desirable outcomes, while mockers will always reinforce poor choices that lead to undesirable consequences. Standing at the center of it all is choice. Got wisdom? Be blessed!

Additional Inspiration: Psalm 19:11

September 10

Proverb 10:22
Wealth

The idea of having wealth does something to us. It is a fantasy and/or a reality that excites many of us. Throughout the Scriptures, Yahweh speaks of wealth and abundance and boasts that He alone is the source of both. We are also instructed to not place our hope in money or material possessions because we cannot faithfully serve two masters, God and money. When we seek God first and sow seed into His kingdom, He promises to reward us. The blessings manifest by increased wealth, peace, health, love, wisdom, promotion, and everything good. Praise God for the promise of more. Amen!

Additional Inspiration: Psalm 118:25–26

September 11

Proverb 11:24
Unduly

Give more and get more is the whole concept here! God keeps promising us throughout the Proverbs that the more we give of ourselves, our time, our talent, and our treasure, the more we get in return. We must be genuine in our giving, of course. God clearly speaks against bribery in all forms and gifts given in secret. Consequences come with those decisions. Likewise when you are able to give and choose to "hold out," that is also a decision that may have negative consequences. Yah says you eventually come to be poor and dependent. Give and live! Shalom!

Additional Inspiration: Psalm 119:36–37

September 12

Proverb 12:23
Folly

Where is the filter? This is such an important Proverb to keep in mind daily as our world becomes increasingly more communicative through various mediums other than face-to-face encounters. We really need to heed Solomon's wisdom, because it can save our lives. If you work or live in a place where there are a lot of people, take time to observe and you will hear a lot of foolishness. With practice, you will find that you can gain value in keeping quiet. Sometimes what God has you to know is just for you and shouldn't be shared. We are our ultimate filter and must take full ownership of this position. Amen!

Additional Inspiration: Psalm 39:1

September 13

Proverb 13:18
Heeds

In a world where we think we can know all the answers, we still manage to find ourselves in situations where mature thinking would be beneficial. Instead we are left in a tight spot where we need advice. Some of us are not willing to open up, be vulnerable, and share, while others of us are excited for feedback and counsel. Our Creator wants us to be aware of our circumstances and to listen when we get council from others and Him.

When we do as we are told and make right choices, we reap the reward, and hence we are honored. When we choose the wrong thing and ignore discipline, we reap the negative consequences or dishonor. Choose wisely and be blessed. Amen!

Additional Inspiration: Psalm 28:1–2

September 14

Proverb 14:29
Patience

Dear friend, we have heard the old adage, "Patience is a virtue," but oftentimes we find it hard to put that statement into action. We operate with a selective patience, meaning we are patient with whom and toward what we choose to be. We all have this inherent ability; however, some possess it more than others. When we exercise patience, we actually perform cognitive therapy on our mind, which in turn benefits our body and spirit. Patience allows us to avoid unnecessary cortisol spikes that occur with stress and tension.

Yahweh says that when we possess understanding, we can allow patience space to activate. When we are foolish we act in silly ways that lead us to be quick-tempered, easily irritated, or negatively aroused. If you fall into the latter category, pray specifically for God to help you be slow to irritation and radiate more with love, patience, and peace. Amen!

Additional Inspiration: Psalm 4:4

Rx: Today be better than you were yesterday and tomorrow better than you are today. ~Dr. J

September 15

Proverb 15:22
Counsel

Praise God for the simple yet powerful promise! Yahweh created us to live out individual uniquely designed plans, yet He created us for community. We are amazingly created beings and as such we are very creative. We sit on many ideas for years, keeping them to ourselves, and the idea goes nowhere. Other times we act naïvely or hastily with ideas only to fizzle out quickly and leave the project unfinished.

But for those who are willing to take a few extra steps to run an idea by Godly counsel, success is waiting. This is an awesome promise! We have to move through the fear as we step out and execute the plans God places on our hearts. Share your ideas with wise counsel, mentors, friends, family, and teachers. Get feedback. Talk with God and then proceed. He won't let you fail. Shalom

Additional Inspiration: Psalm 4:1

September 16

Proverb 16:25
Seems

"Things aren't always what they seem" goes the old adage. This Proverb highlights this truth perfectly. Situations and circumstances and even people can appear to look or be one way but turn out to be different than what you thought. This of course can come with little to no consequences, while in other instances, as the Proverb indicates, the consequences can lead to death.

Ultimately we are all going to pass away, but we can lessen the likelihood of an untimely death by making better life choices. Remember that we can experience a death of dreams, ideas, opportunities, and connections all due to inaccurate planning. We can confidently consult with God for everything. He desires to show us the way to the finish line of the race He has marked out for us to run. Be blessed!

Additional Inspiration: Psalm 22:11

Rx: Today be better than you were yesterday and tomorrow better than you are today. ~Dr. J

September 17

Proverb 17:22
Spirit

The mind, body, and soul tripartite is a powerful relationship that must be considered in more detail. It is overwhelming when we ponder how highly integrated the systems within us are. We live in a culture that tries to treat bodily ailments with chemical or physical solutions. Oftentimes, as this Proverb indicates, the medicine needed is a spiritual or emotional prescription. The opposite of dry brittle bones, a weak foundation, are lubricated joints and strong bones, a firm foundation. Don't let your attitude dictate your health. Pray, repent, forgive, forgive again, and move on. Selah!

Additional Inspiration: Psalm 51:7–8

September 18

Proverb 18:16
Gift

Giving gifts is great, but this is not an excuse to go out and shop. ;-) What Yahweh wants us to understand is the power of generosity and a giving spirit. Notice the writer never mentions the price of the gift or what type of gift. We can give of ourselves with our time, talent, and/or treasure. Of course, the caveat is being genuine in our action. God knows our heart and sees our intentions and motives. The point is that there is positive spiritual energy that is released through our physical acts of kindness. So go ahead and get giving. Amen!

Additional Inspiration: Psalm 100:4–5

Rx: Today be better than you were yesterday and tomorrow better than you are today. ~Dr. J

September 19

Proverb 19:20
Accept

Why is this so hard for some of us to do? Listening is an art and skill that one must master. Our attention spans are minimal, and oftentimes we just want to air what we want to say. Once we master listening, we then must learn what to do with the information we receive. We cannot merely listen to instruction for it to be useful; we must also act on it.

This process of listening, accepting, believing, and acting can yield good and bad results depending on whom we are listening to and the choices we make. Be ever so cautious of whom you accept instruction from. God is clear that we should get advice from wise counselors, men, and women who have an honest relationship with God. Worldly wisdom has no standing against Spiritual wisdom of the Holy Spirit. You can trust Yahweh to lead you to the right people and put you on the right path. Shalom!

Additional Inspiration: Psalm 119:66

September 20

Proverb 20:22
Wait

If you have ever been the victim of someone's mal-intent and you felt the need to retaliate out of restoring justice, this Proverb is for you. When we harbor an evil plan and deceit in our heart, we are no better than the person who offended us. We of course must call authorities for major criminal activity and let them handle it. This Proverb is referring to a victim taking the law into his or her own hands. Don't block your blessings by playing the role of avenger in your life. Let Jehovah Rapha avenge on your behalf. He knows, He cares, and He is always on it. Amen!

Additional Inspiration: Psalm 27:14

September 21

Proverb 21:23
Calamity

We obviously need to communicate with one another, right? It is an absolute in order to work together in community. Yet, we find daily communication to be one of our biggest challenges. How we listen, how we speak, and how we come across are or are not at the forefront of our minds throughout the day. Either we choose to be ourselves while being careful not to offend or we choose to be ourselves and not care if we offend others with our speech and actions.

When we examine this Proverb, it makes the idea of word choice much more appealing. No one desires unfortunate catastrophic events to happen unto themselves. That is truly calamity! If it can be brought on by what we verbalize, then it is wise that we keep watch and protect against potential danger. Let's think before we speak. Amen!

Additional Inspiration: Psalm 139:4

September 22

Proverb 22:18
Ready

Here is the million-dollar secret to making God smile: simply be obedient to His word. You are thinking, "That's it?" Yes, that's it! Jah states over and over again that He requires us to be prudent, self-controlled, loving, and forgiving beings. When we get with God on a regular basis through our devotional time, He is ecstatic.

We learn in this passage that God is pleased with us when we keep (commit to memory) His instruction and have it ready for use (can apply it). This is something we can easily test and see that God is good. Don't be discouraged or lose heart on this journey with El Elyon. We serve a mighty God who only desires good for us. Keep moving forward and press on toward the goal. Amen!

Additional Inspiration: Psalm 119:43–44

Rx: Today be better than you were yesterday and tomorrow better than you are today. ~Dr. J

September 23

Proverb 23:22
Despise

Although we are not living under the law because of the courageous love Yeshua showed us on the cross, we still ought to be wise and honor the 10 Commandments of which Yahweh came to fulfill. Friends, God gave us these pointers to help us, not harm us. They offer a guide on how to live and they give life when we put them into action. This Proverb takes us to Commandment No. 5, "Thou shall honor thy mother and father." Obviously this is going to look different for each of us because we all have unique circumstances with our parents. Whenever possible, always look to be at peace and respect your parents. God understands the rest. Be blessed!

Additional Inspiration: Psalm 78:1–4

September 24

Proverb 24:26
Honest

Let's keep it real! It is often hard to let truth prevail. True, honesty is the best policy, but we often find it hard to simply tell someone they have food stuck in between their teeth or food on their face. When we do step out of our comfort zone and give someone a heads up about such a thing, they are usually thankful. Recognizing that the truth can hurt, we must always be mindful of our delivery and the presence of others. The Word says, "Iron sharpens iron." When we love one another and are honest, we grow mentally, spiritually, and physically. Let's keep keeping it real!

Additional Inspiration: Psalm 31:14

September 25

Proverb 25:21-22
Enemy

Although we have been given the command to love one another, God's word clearly illustrates that not everyone will be our friend. The statement "We can't be everything to everyone" is not pessimistic; it is indeed realistic. We have to face the fact that even on our best days when we feel we are the nicest person in the world, we (yes, you!) can still get on others' nerves or someone may get under our skin, leaving you at odds with them. An enemy is not a friend, and out of envy, jealousy, bitterness, or anger, you may experience their energy.

The best way to deal with someone who has not treated you right or is not an ally is to extend love. It sounds crazy, but in this Proverb, Yah promises to reward us for this type of behavior. I kind of want the reward — don't you? If you trust Him, trust His word and do what it says. Shalom!

Additional Inspiration: Psalm 18:24-26

Rx: Today be better than you were yesterday and tomorrow better than you are today. ~Dr. J

September 26

Proverb 26:17
Medals

In this Proverb, Yah gives us a very clear description of what not to get into. Most of us would not go up to an unknown dog and seize it by the ears. Innately, most of us would be afraid of getting bitten by the dog. This may be true even if we know the dog. God likens this unsafe situation to getting involved in other people's business. Learn to keep boundaries.

If you see people arguing, it is best to call the authorities and not to get personally involved. You could end up hurt or worsen the situation by your actions or comments. This is obviously a personal decision, but it is biblical. Pray about it and be safe. Shalom!

Additional Inspiration: Psalm 65:4

Rx: Today be better than you were yesterday and tomorrow better than you are today. ~Dr. J

September 27

Proverb 27:18
Honored

Simply put, you will be rewarded for a job well done. If you didn't get the memo, you are purposed for a mission that Yahweh has designed uniquely for you. We all have our own thing going on! This is why the list of possible professions seems endless and people are conducting work everywhere. Contained on that same memo, however, is God's warning to us if we don't use our gifts. Let it be known that Yahweh dislikes laziness; it is detestable to Him.

When we work we actually bring health to our mind, body, and spirit. God is our Creator, and we in turn also create. How awesomely made are we? Supercalifragilisticexpialidocious awesome! Remember this verse when you wonder why you have to work. Because you will indeed get paid and then you can eat, pay your bills, and bless others. You honor God with your service. Amen!

Additional Inspiration: Psalm 59:17

September 28

Proverb 28:22
Poverty

You may recognize the motto here of "Give more, get more in return" or "You reap what you sow." When we express and nurture good energy, positive thoughts, and healing actions in our circle of influence, the law of Yahweh says that we will reap a bountiful harvest. God doesn't repay good with evil. When we are stingy, that often stems from a place of insecurity and worry that we may be without.

We have to be willing to trust God and let go of some things that hold us and that we also hold too tight. After all, everything we have already belongs to God, and He can take it at any time. We should not be afraid to give. God loves and rewards a cheerful giver. Test Him and see. Shalom!

Additional Inspiration: Psalm 9:16–18

Rx: Today be better than you were yesterday and tomorrow better than you are today. ~Dr. J

September 29

Proverb 29:17
Discipline

Discipline is good for our spiritual, mental, and physical health. This Proverb speaks about sons, but it applies to daughters as well. In fact, we can extrapolate and apply this message to our entire lifetime journey. Discipline, obedience, and taking action are keys to life successes. Consider how Yahweh encourages us to think of discipline and peace as a chain reaction. Don't you see this in your life? When you set out to accomplish the goals placed before you, you feel at peace. You feel productive and there is delight in your soul.

We see this cycle played out daily. We also see the opposite and we know all too well the way it feels when we miss the mark and fail to stay disciplined to accomplish our goals. Since we have a choice, let's choose wisely. Always try to remember how good your soul delight feels when you win. Shalom!

Additional Inspiration: Psalm 94:12-13

Rx: Today be better than you were yesterday and tomorrow better than you are today. ~Dr. J

September 30

Proverb 30:20
Adulteress

Dear friends, if we consider an adulteress to be someone or something that is out of covenant with God, then we can easily extrapolate and apply this verse to many areas of our lives. The adulteress shows up in our person, families, workplaces, government, media/advertising, education, and more. Almost any sector across the globe, anywhere there are human beings, the work of the liar is there.

One of the hallmarks of the adversary is taking the posture of arrogance that nothing is wrong with evil conduct and it is simply our freedom of choice. It is a pattern of thought that reflects in a way of life. How we conduct ourselves speaks volumes to our thought life. Pray and ask Yah to transform your thought life so that you can continue to withstand the adulterous flare that so dominates the world. Shalom!

Additional Inspiration: Psalm 32:10–11

Rx: Today be better than you were yesterday and tomorrow better than you are today. ~Dr. J

OCTOBER

From the fruit of his mouth a man's stomach is filled; with the harvest from his lips he is satisfied.

Proverb 18:20

October 1

Proverb 1:31
Fruit

We have heard the sayings "What goes around comes around" and "You reap what you sow"; it is easy to think of some grandiose offense that these sayings apply to. Give it no further thought; in this passage God is warning us of exactly that. We serve a God who cares about grandiose, as much as little sin.

In fact He sees it all the same and reserves the same punishment for it all. When we don't listen to Him, we communicate that we don't care. Think about that for a minute. When we face the consequences, aka "the fruit" of our poor choices, we should not be surprised. Every day make an effort to live wisely and in peace. Amen!

Additional Inspiration: Psalm 125:4–5

October 2

Proverb 2:20
Righteous

Dear friends, we have a choice: either we walk with God or we walk without Him. Sometimes we want to straddle the fence, but ultimately that never works well for a productive future and can leave us feeling stagnant and confused. Yah promises us life, honor, and prosperity when we seek and act with good intentions. This is the path of the righteous and the way of good humans, and the reward is ours for the taking. Think about the kind of person you want to be and how you want to be remembered after you leave earth. Pray daily and ask God to guide your steps. Press in, press on, and be blessed!

Additional Inspiration: Psalm 18:36

October 3

Proverb 3:26–27
Withhold

We can easily question ourselves when it comes to giving freely to others. Why is that? Sometimes we question what the homeless person would do with the money or if we can trust our friend or relative to pay us back the money he or she just asked to borrow. We even question the validity of honoring those who do good works. Why is this so?

Here God tells us when we are able to we should freely give to those who have earned it or who need it. The next time your spirit prompts you to give or to honor someone, don't let the enemy steal the opportunity for you to brighten another person's day. Shalom!

Additional Inspiration: Psalm 112:5

October 4

Proverb 4:23
Wellspring

Dear friend, one of the most important tasks we have is to get our mind right. We only fool ourselves if we think we can make wise, Godly decisions when our minds are sick. Yahweh tells us a person's character is revealed from their heart. So, how do we upright our thinking? It begins with a daily renewal of our mind. How we live our life, what we think, say, listen to, and do all revolve around our character.

Understanding and facing the junk that's in our heart can certainly prompt us to make necessary adjustments so we can be our best selves. None of this is selfish. It is actually selfless because when we are our best selves, we can be better for others. Similar to the safety instructions on an airplane, only after securing your own air mask first can you then help someone else. Let's think, pray, and be blessed today. Amen!

Additional Inspiration: Psalm 86:11

Rx: Today be better than you were yesterday and tomorrow better than you are today. ~Dr. J

October 5

Proverb 5:21
View

Out of sight, out of mind—so the saying goes. Just because we can't see Him, doesn't mean He doesn't know. El Elyon makes it clear throughout Scripture that He indeed sees us—from the Psalms, where Jehovah describes fastening us in our mother's womb, to Jeremiah, where He professes to have specific plans for us. Although this may be a little unnerving at first thought, as we mature in our faith and reverence for Him, we will care more about what He thinks. This will cause us to examine our ways and, in turn, make adjustments purely out of our love for Him. What an awesome God we serve!

Additional Inspiration: Psalm 119:168

October 6

Proverb 6:23
Correction

When we consider the idea that we are under spiritual training, it may be easier to accept the notion that we need commands and corrections from our certified personal trainer, Yahweh. This is a true blessing, and the earlier we enact it, the more we will live out our spiritual calling. How often do we have anxiety over "the way we should go"? If only we had a crystal ball. The truth is we do. His word, teaching, love, discipline, and rebuke guides us. Proverbs are a lamp unto our feet. He will show us how and where to take our next step. Hallelujah!

Additional Inspiration: Psalm 43:3

Rx: Today be better than you were yesterday and tomorrow better than you are today. ~Dr. J

October 7

Proverb 7:24
Listen

Have you ever been so focused on what you were watching or listening to that you didn't want to be interrupted? If someone would try to talk to you, you might signal that they wait because you don't want to miss the one word or scene. This, my friend, is the level of intentional listening Yah encourages us to have for His direction and teaching. In fact, God commands us over and over again in the Scriptures to listen and pay attention to His words. The fact that He says it repeatedly gives insight to the level of importance. Let's not miss this in our spiritual walk. Keep our eyes, ears, and minds steady on Him. Be blessed!

Additional Inspiration: Psalm 27:11

October 8

Proverb 8:30–31
Craftsman

Every bit of creation is alive, and we all share in this mind-boggling experience. It is mind-altering to think that wisdom herself had delight and rejoiced in creating with God. These are emotions and actions we can relate to. Yahweh has assignments for us, and He wants us to find joy in our toil. Let us praise Him for His supernatural carpentry and that we can live with delight and rejoice as we do our work unto Him. Shalom!

Additional Inspiration: Psalm 24:1–2

Rx: Today be better than you were yesterday and tomorrow better than you are today. ~Dr. J

October 9

Proverb 9:13-14
Good

The typical American movie always has the good versus evil theme, which parallels the reality of the world. Both good and evil are coexisting on our planet, in our universe, atmosphere, our homes, workspaces, academic institutions, governments, friendships, businesses, and marriages. God will elevate both the fools and the wise to pillars of success. Folly sits at the door of her house on a seat at the highest point of the city.

So, don't be surprised when you see fools in all the high places; the Bible already told you it would be so. Remember that Yahweh is the Most High and sits at the highest point. Trust that God will restore justice and balance one day. Shalom!

Additional Inspiration: Psalm 83:18

October 10

Proverb 10:23
Fool

The facts are what they are, and we live in a world where evil and foolish people exist. When you consider that some people find pleasure in evil conduct, the truth is even more disturbing. There may be ways that seem right to us, but according to God, those ways lead to death. If you find yourself enjoying behaviors and activities that are unholy, continue to keep those things in prayer.

Don't feel trapped. When we begin to mature in our relationship with Yahweh, we will develop a taste for righteous living. Pray for the fruit of wisdom and self-control. Be blessed!

Additional Inspiration: Psalm 119:101–103

October 11

Proverb 11:25
Refreshed

Give and expect something in return. It's biblical to think this way and have this expectation. God wants us to give to others with the use of our time, talent, and resources. When we take time to be generous and care for one another, Yahweh promises us that we will prosper. Of course we want to approach this with the right motive and intention, not with a heart of bribery or buying affection. Yah rewards the intention behind the action. El Elyon has given us all our unique sets of gifts and abilities from which we get to serve the world. Within these realms is where our mission awaits. Amen!

Additional Inspiration: Psalm 112:4

October 12

Proverb 12:24
Desire

If you don't desire to work hard for yourself, you will end up working hard for someone else. If you don't desire to work hard for someone else, you will more than likely face poverty. Hands that stay busy working on projects that produce profit will reap a harvest. This is a promise that Yahweh makes to us, and God keeps His promises. This should both excite and motivate us.

Remember getting allowance as a kid and being excited about the monetary reward, treats, or fun outing? Our anticipation for the reward allowed us to complete our chores. Just as our earthly parents rewarded us for our work, Jehovah wants to bless us even more for our labor. Let's make God proud and keep doing good works to bring Him glory. Shalom!

Additional Inspiration: Psalm 37:5–6

Rx: Today be better than you were yesterday and tomorrow better than you are today. ~Dr. J

October 13

Proverb 13:19
Longing

Yahweh has deposited dreams and desires into each and every one of us humans. These spiritual downloads are our vision and give way to our purpose. He does this to bring glory to Himself as He manifests His will through us. If you have ever accomplished the task that you had been working on for hours, days, weeks, months, or years, you know the sweet feeling of satisfaction from completing the task. God designed us this way. When we are foolish and allow evil to persist in our lives, we miss out on fulfilling our purpose for God. Our soul never tastes the sweetness it was designed to savor. Read Ecclesiastes 2:13 and 2:26. Selah!

Additional Inspiration: Psalm 20:5

Rx: Today be better than you were yesterday and tomorrow better than you are today. ~Dr. J

October 14

Proverb 14:30
Rot

Have you ever wondered why we are seeing a rise in diseases with an unknown cause? We live in a world where we see an increasing amount of allergies, autoimmune disorders, and behavioral health diagnoses that medical experts can't give clear explanations regarding the cause. Our Creator knows the source of all our sufferings, and we know that we serve a healing God.

Sometimes the source of our diagnosis is coming from our thought life, and since our thoughts our invisible, it is no wonder the medical doctors can't give us a clear explanation. Obviously this is not everyone's reason for their condition, but for many it is. We have to acknowledge the power of the invisible forms of negative energy that can kill us such as pride, bitterness, jealousy, hate, arrogance, and envy. God is clear there are consequences to our thoughts as well as our actions.

A heart of peace can bring life to your body. Rotting bones lend to the image of brittle bones—osteoporosis—which can greatly limit your ability to move and be free. Peace is our prescription, and there is no co-pay required. Shalom!

Additional Inspiration: Psalm 49:16–17

Rx: Today be better than you were yesterday and tomorrow better than you are today. ~Dr. J

October 15

Proverb 15:23
Apt

Have you ever experienced hearing a message that sounded like it was just for you? What about a conversation with a friend and they just spoke the word you needed to hear? How awesome are these one-off experiences! At the moment you feel as if the universe perhaps collaborated to bring the divine appointment. Well, there is truth there. We are a reflection of our Creator, and His word is always timely and spot on. Look and listen for God to speak to you through people and situations, as well as His word. Stay prayed up! Be blessed today and always.

Additional Inspiration: Psalm 5:1–3

October 16

Proverb 16:26
Appetite

Have you been so hungry that you could not focus on anything except acquiring food? What about a life goal or project? Have you ever experienced a desire for an opportunity that it propelled you forward? This Proverb shows us how to maintain our momentum and drive by staying hungry. Don't get so full and satiated that you get lazy and do not want to push forward. Staying hungry is the catalyst for growth and change.

The laborer's appetite, his or her hunger, and the desire to fulfill gives the laborer the motivation to keep working, make a profit, and get the project done. In the end the reward is all theirs. What are you hungry or desiring for? Keep pressing forward and use that insatiable feeling to fuel you to meet your goals. God will bless and reward you for your steps of progress. Be blessed!

Additional Inspiration: Psalm 18:32–33

Rx: Today be better than you were yesterday and tomorrow better than you are today. ~Dr. J

October 17

Proverb 17:24
Wander

We definitely live in a time where anything goes. With the advance of technology and all sorts of information literally at our fingertips, we can easily wander to the ends of the earth and back in just a few clicks. Many people feel purposeless and find themselves starting a new hobby, project, job, or relationship only to lose interest in a short time. We simply fizzle out. Amen if this has ever been your experience. Luckily we have a solution hand-tailored for this.

According to Yahweh, when we practice discerning and understanding, we are able to keep wisdom in full view. This means we can operate with intentional purpose. God is not the author of confusion, and He desires for us to know and live out our purpose. Ask, seek, and knock, and the door will be opened to you. Shalom!

Additional Inspiration: Psalm 16:6

October 18

Proverb 18:20
Harvest

We have the power to speak blessings and prosperity over our life. The God we serve is a God of increase. By His mouth He spoke the world as we know it into existence. By His mouth and lips, He breathed the breath of life into us, His creation. Hallelujah and by the power of the Holy Spirit living within us, we have that same power to speak life over ourselves and our family. Praise Yah! This isn't about being arrogant or boastful, but rather owning a positive self-esteem. Every day we must believe and declare everything good over our life. Amen!

Additional Inspiration: Psalm 18:1–2

October 19

Proverb 19:21
Prevail

Yah's way is always better! This nugget of wisdom is repeated multiple times in the Proverbs, suggesting a high level of importance for us to understand in our continued growth with God. He places desires in our heart and wants us to pursue those things He has purposed for us with all our might. He rewards those skillful at their work and who are diligent with their hands and time.

We serve a God who has a plan into which we fit. Therefore, we must be flexible and know that no matter what desires are or are not being fulfilled in our lives right now, His ways are indeed higher than ours. It is His kingdom come and His will be done. He has our back, always. Shalom!

Additional Inspiration: Psalm 139:16

October 20

Proverb 20:23 and 20:10
Detest

Does injustice anger you and get under your skin? Don't be alarmed if you find that to be one of your triggers. Injustice and dishonesty anger God, too. According to this verse, it is detestable to Him. When you see unfair situations erupting around us, remember to pray and don't ever let it waver your faith in the Almighty. Please believe He sees and is displeased.

The Holy Spirit groans and moans for us, just as Jesus died for us, so we can choose better. Ultimately human beings have the freedom to choose their behavior. No matter how dishonest and turned up the people of the world may become, we should never let it dictate our faith in Jehovah. Amen!

Additional Inspiration: Psalm 106:3

Rx: Today be better than you were yesterday and tomorrow better than you are today. ~Dr. J

October 21

Proverb 21:25-26
Craves

Got fruit? We all have our share of wants and desires. When we have craved something and had that desire met, we experience satisfaction and pleasure. When we hope for something and it never materializes or eludes us, it actually affects our emotions. We lose a sense of purpose and can easily become depressed or discouraged.

One sure way to circumvent this from reoccurring in our lives is to keep active and connect with God daily in prayer about it. Laziness will result in us not being active and not yielding the results we want so badly to achieve. If we really want to see fruit in our lives, there is no other option. Stay motivated. Amen!

Additional Inspiration: Psalm 143:4-5

October 22

Proverb 22:24–25
Hot-Tempered

Anger is contagious. Is this why God tells us to not even associate with a hot-tempered person? Scripture tells us to be slow to anger and irritability. However, we see that God becomes angry throughout the Word. We must remember to keep all this in perspective and context. Think for a moment what Yahweh gets upset about, and notice the similarity within us. We are easily angered about social injustice or crimes against humanity. But to just be angry at the world or a person who explodes requires further examination.

When we get angry irrationally, we are very emotionally charged and oftentimes we don't approach people or situations in a problem-solving fashion due to the presence of that irrational anger. Remember the charge given to us by Jesus that we should live at peace with one another at all times, as much as possible. Amen!

Additional Inspiration: Psalm 7:15–17

Rx: Today be better than you were yesterday and tomorrow better than you are today. ~Dr. J

October 23

Proverb 23:23
Truth

Wisdom, discipline, understanding, and truth—this is a mouthful! How do we attain these things? Even if we have to spend money to get it, Yahweh says, just do it and not to resell it. We are to keep it so we can use it over and over again. When we buy a book to help us learn habits or to study the Scriptures, God wants us to dig deep and not just let the information go in one ear and out the other. This requires discipline. Friends, when we decide to think better and do better, we will see more miracles in our life. Retrain your brain to love the life you live. Be blessed!

Additional Inspiration: Psalm 116:1–2

October 24

Proverb 24:27
Build

Ready, set, go! God gives us a pattern for life in the Scriptures. When we read and apply the principles, it takes a lot of guesswork out of the decision-making process. We begin to recognize that there is an order and a priority to life. The first action this Proverb tells us to take is external preparation. We must actively plan for harvest. This is not a passive process. Get your field ready and lay your foundation on solid rock. Trust it all unto Yeshua. After this, you can build a house that will last. Remember, it is preparation that precedes blessing. Let's think!

Additional Inspiration: Psalm 111:5–7

Rx: Today be better than you were yesterday and tomorrow better than you are today. ~Dr. J

October 25

Proverb 25:23
Sly

Being quick-witted and being abrasive are two different things. The typical "smart aleck" is one many of us don't desire to be around. Some people are quick-witted and bring humor to a situation. Very quickly, when the same reply is applied in a way that is demeaning or insinuates something bad, we pick up on it instantly, and it is not a pleasant feeling. This is part of our creative design. Our words have power, and we must remember to err on the side of caution when we speak. Focus on thinking before speaking and remember: speak peace to keep peace. Shalom!

Additional Inspiration: Psalm 12:3–4

October 26

Proverb 26:20
Gossip

Have you ever encountered a person or group of people who seem to always keep drama stirred up? This isn't something that occurs by accident. Some people are inclined to start fires. We can think of gossips and quarrel starters as spiritual pyromaniacs. Fire has multiple purposes that benefit us, such as warmth, light, cooking food, and purification.

However, unquenched, unwanted, uncontrolled fires are life-threatening. The more fuel and wood added, the more damage. If you are someone who is inclined to gossip and quarrel, it is time for change. Be honest with yourself and offer it to God in prayer. Selah!

Additional Inspiration: Psalm 52:3–4

October 27

Proverb 27:19
Reflects

Have you heard the saying, "You wear your emotions on your sleeve"? Well, this tongue-in-cheek expression has a root in this verse. Jesus taught that our heart condition is reflected in our actions. We commit adultery the moment we lust in our heart or murder another the minute we think that offensive thought in our mind towards a person. From out of a man's heart, so he speaks. The comparison made here to our face reflected in water should make it clear to us that we are not fooling anyone, especially not Yahweh. We all need a heart monitor, called Jesus, to help us with this. Ask God to change your heart condition. Remember, it is a process, and we are being transformed for His glory. Amen!

Additional Inspiration: Psalm 43:5

October 28

Proverb 28:23
Flattering

Many of us hate being told what to do or being corrected. While we may happily welcome self-improvement strategies, we often would prefer that they be self-initiated rather than initiated by others. Something literally feels out of sync within our body when we hear someone tell us we are wrong–when we experience rebuke. Yet when someone flatters us, we feel great—some of us shyly perhaps, but internally we feel awesome.

Flattery invisibly puffs us up, while rebuke invisibly deflates us. According to El Shaddai, we should approach this differently. We should feel good about telling the truth and doing what is right before God. Be cautious when someone gives you too many compliments, and take heed when someone corrects you in love. This is how we grow and gain favor with the Lord. It's all about transformation. Amen!

Additional Inspiration: Psalm 5:9

Rx: Today be better than you were yesterday and tomorrow better than you are today. ~Dr. J

October 29

Proverb 29:20
Haste

Our mouths can get us into a whole bunch of trouble. We need to understand the power of spoken word. God spoke, and because we are made in His image, we speak. We have the ability to declare, as our Creator declared, with intention, precision, and purpose. We must be mindful of what we say. When we are hasty, we may say or do things that can have severe consequences. There is so much written in the Scriptures about speaking. Do we need to wonder why? Selah and Shalom!

Additional Inspiration: Psalm 36:2–3

October 30

Proverb 30:24-25
Wise

Yah instructs us to be good stewards of our time, talent, and treasure. Everything that we have is a gift from God, and we must treat it as such. Yahweh tells us to observe the wisdom of an ant, a creature very weak compared to the environment in which it lives. Ants demonstrate stewardship by storing up food in summer so they are prepared for the cold months ahead. Friends, are we not called to the same wisdom, the same stewardship? We are indeed!

We ought to save our money, develop our gifts, share with the needy, and invest. When we invest in ourselves, our children, and others, we all get better, together. When the winter hits, we will be prepared, together. Be blessed!

Additional Inspiration: Psalm 39:6-7

October 31

Proverb 31:27
Idleness

A steward is given the responsibility of watching over his or her affairs. We all have a dominion that we have been given to reside over. How we care for it is our choice. If we decide that we don't want to clean our house, yet we can't hire someone to do it for us, our house will become dirty with dust, ants, maggots, fungus, mold, and mildew due to stagnation.

When we are running in neutral, we are not making progress, and we don't grow. Remaining in the same stagnant position, we easily become susceptible to spiritual, physical, and mental ills. Let's meditate and pray about this. Be aware of your level of stewardship and stay active. Amen!

Additional Inspiration: Psalm 90:16–17

NOVEMBER

There is no wisdom, no insight, no plan
that can succeed against the Lord.
Proverb 21:30

November 1

Proverb 1:32
Complacent

It only takes one major or a collection of a few minor poor choices to have our entire little world turned upside down. Thoughts such as "If only I had known," "I wish I had known," or "If I could do it again, I would" are all too common in daily dialogue with friends, family, colleagues, acquaintances, people on TV, and even within our own mind. It is fair to say that human beings grapple with freedom of choice.

The unique gift Yahweh has given us can destroy us if we use it incorrectly. Living a complacent life and practicing activities, thoughts, dialogue, and habits that are wayward will ultimately bring harm upon us and lead to death of dreams and opportunities. Thank God we can choose right. With His help our little world can be full of life. Hallelujah!

Additional Inspiration: Psalm 53:1

November 2

Proverb 2:21
Upright

Dear Friend, remember that we are covered by the blood of Jesus Christ and that we have been made right in the eyes of the Lord through our acceptance of Yeshua Hamashiach. However, we should never take these gifts of mercy and grace for granted. We still have a duty to align our behaviors, thoughts, and motives with that of our Creator. We are in the process of transformation, and consequently, we will experience times when we are not acting, thinking, or speaking in a way that pleases God.

The good news is that as we grow and become increasingly self-aware, we can quickly detect this misalignment, confess it, and ask Jah to empower us to not act, speak, or think that way again. We must be patient with ourselves and others. We are under spiritual reconstruction. Shalom!

Additional Inspiration: Psalm 27:13

Rx: Today be better than you were yesterday and tomorrow better than you are today. ~Dr. J

November 3

Proverb 3:28
Respect

This verse indicates that a mutual level of inherent trust and respect must exist between neighbors, friends, colleagues, and frankly anyone with whom we have relationships. It is much easier to be upright and honest. When we borrow from someone, that person should never have to come looking for us to return the item, money, or whatever. If we want to coexist in harmony with one another and desire to help one another to reach our shared and individual dreams, it is imperative that we be women and men of our word. Amen!

Additional Inspiration: Psalm 109:3–5

November 4

Proverb 4:24
Perversity

Common phrases such as "Think positive" and "You are what you think" are no doubt true and impactful statements that have motivated many of us to change. In addition to being mindful of what we think about, we also need to consider what we talk about. The words we speak add another layer of power to us humans. Speaking truth and keeping falsehood and lies far from our lips adds health to our body.

Speak love and life into one another, not death. Speak education and inspiration into each other's lives. These healing conversations will reduce stress and promote wellness. Pray Yahweh guide us in being more aware of what we say and to make adjustments as needed. Sometimes this includes us apologizing if we have hurt someone with our words. Shalom!

Additional Inspiration: Psalm 4:24

Rx: Today be better than you were yesterday and tomorrow better than you are today. ~Dr. J

November 5

Proverb 5:22
Ensnare

This verse may sound gloomy to us, but it shouldn't. We ought to be thankful that we serve a just God, one who cares enough to give us instructions in proper living and rewards those who choose to go in the Way. Yahweh makes it clear that evil will face severe consequences. While it is definitely hard for us to believe this, especially as we see the world turned up around us, we must have faith in His promises. Sin is an infectious trap that causes spiritual bankruptcy.

If you have ever struggled with stopping a bad or undesirable behavior, you understand the hold evil can have. Pray without ceasing and let God be the focus. He works everything for the good of those who love Him. Amen!

Additional Inspiration: Psalm 58:1–3

November 6

Proverb 6:27-28
Scorched

This seems so obvious to us, yet we do this spiritually and emotionally much of the time. There is a small group of people who like to experience physical pain: masochists. However, most of us want to avoid things that will bring us physical pain and deformation. We must be as diligent with applying this practice if we are to lessen our experience with spiritual and emotional pain. We cannot escape it altogether because it is part of life, but we can minimize scorching experiences by making better choices. That's really all we have, folks. Trust and follow God. Peace!

Additional Inspiration: Psalm 11:7

November 7

Proverb 7:25
Stray

We are first warned to not let our hearts turn to the ways of the unwise and foolish. We are then cautioned to not stray onto the paths of the unwise and foolish. Yahweh makes this distinction because our decisions first manifest in our heart. From our emotional centers, the heart and mind, we give birth to action, whether sin or righteousness. They are birthed in the same place.

Once we rationalize an idea in our mind, we then engage in the chosen behavior. Hence the instruction to not stray onto the wrong path; the choice is ours. We must keep our heart and mind in check at any and all cost. Choose the good, choose life, and choose God. Amen!

Additional Inspiration: Psalm 26:2–4

November 8

Proverb 8:33–34
Listen

The only way we can know Yah is to read His Word. The only way we can become who He is calling us to be is through practical application of what we hear and read. If we read the Word of God out loud, we can in a sense listen to Yah. Practice reading the Proverbs out loud and ask God to speak to you. He gives freely wisdom to those who ask. When we read the Scriptures, He tells us how to find wisdom. Be aware, listen, watch, and wait. Over time and with practice, we will become more sensitive to our helper, the Holy Spirit. Amen!

Additional Inspiration: Psalm 25:10

November 9

Proverb 9:4 and 9:16
Simple

This verse is repeated twice in Proverb 9 and with good reason. Yahweh really wants us to learn this principle. The world will call out to you and tempt you in many different ways, appealing to all your senses. In some ways media and advertising use the psychology of humans to get us to buy their products. If it didn't work, companies wouldn't spend billions of dollars annually in the form of radio, print, digital, and televised ads.

I'm not saying that we should not advertise, because it is a part of business. Yet it is to say: be on guard at all times. We are told in the book of James that the enemy, Satan, prowls and lurks around looking for those to devour. Seek God on everything and make decisions with Godly counsel. Selah!

Additional Inspiration: Psalm 19:8

November 10

Proverb 10:24
Righteous

When you accept Jesus Christ as your savior and begin committing your life to living as He lived (praying, meditating, loving, forgiving, serving, etc.), we become righteous in the eyes of Jehovah. This is grace! We are not perfect and will continue to make mistakes until we die, but Yeshua saved us while we were and are still sinners. We are righteous due to our posture toward God and our belief in Jesus.

He promises that our desires will be granted. This is quite an offer, one we should all take advantage of. You may not feel worthy, but El Elyon says you are. He wants to bless us abundantly. So be bold and just ask Him. Selah!

Additional Inspiration: Psalm 21:2

November 11

Proverb 11:27
Goodwill

Don't go looking for trouble because you will find it indeed. It is just as easy to find trouble to get involved with as it is to find good things to be engaged in. We have the divine given ability to choose, a gift that should be taken seriously. No doubt, life isn't perfect, and we will have trouble, trials, and tribulations. When they come, Yahweh is here to guide and protect us.

We can use a gauge to help assess our choices, behaviors, thoughts, and actions. Simply ask yourself, "Is this 'xyz' thought, action, behavior, pleasing to God?" You will usually know the answer when you get honest with yourself. When we choose God's way, we can and should live with great expectation. Be Blessed!

Additional Inspiration: Psalm 34:8

November 12

Proverb 12:25
Anxious

Anxiousness has had its place among humans from the beginning. It is normal to be concerned about our lives, our family, finances, friends, world affairs, and so on. When we let these worries consume our thoughts and actions and interfere with our daily living, it is problematic. Not only should we consider speaking to a behavioral health professional, we should also present our request and petitions before Jehovah. He has the power to heal us from all our worries and fears.

Jesus tells us to take His yoke upon us because it is light. This is what it means to cast your cares on Him. Yes it's easier said than done, but you won't experience relief until you try. We also have the responsibility to speak kind words to one another, especially when we observe a need. Drop the stress and be blessed!

Additional Inspiration: Psalm 94:18–19

November 13

Proverb 13:20
Companion

You're never too old to succumb to peer pressure. Be aware of your surroundings and the company you keep. This is easy to consider when we think of our children and whom we would or wouldn't want them hanging around. Yet for us adults, it can be much more difficult to put into practice. After all, we are adults and we got this, right?

Unfortunately, we are all sheep and easily led astray. There are many references to this in the Scriptures. Bad brings good down much quicker than good bringing bad up. It is a very elementary way to think of it, but it is a simple, life-saving truth. We are like the company we keep. Choose your friends wisely, and you will be rewarded. Shalom!

Additional Inspiration: Psalm 101:3–4

November 14

Proverb 14:31
Contempt

If we could wrap our minds around the concept of this Proverb and fully embrace it, many of our humanitarian causes would not be required. This Proverb is the crux to a loving relationship with God. When people are held back from becoming who they are designed to be, free with choice and opportunity, they experience oppression. Oppression occurs at various socioeconomic levels across sectors and ethnic groups and with varying magnitude.

When it is done to those who cannot afford to stand up for themselves, it results in some of the most horrific crimes against humanity that we have seen throughout global history. Look at this through the lens of Jehovah and know that when we disrespect the underserved, we disrespect God. Moreover, when we love on those in need, we glorify the Lord Almighty. It's imperative we give more thought to our ways. Selah!

Additional Inspiration: Psalm 109:30–31

Rx: Today be better than you were yesterday and tomorrow better than you are today. ~Dr. J

November 15

Proverb 15:30
Cheerful

Censor what you say and watch your display! It's amazing the depth of things that can have an effect on our body. It's easy to consider the effects of physical activity or foods we consume as having a direct impact on our health, but here in this Proverb, Yahweh is teaching us that our emotional state has a direct impact on our body as well. With this knowledge, we must then be intentional about monitoring our emotions and how we allow others' emotions to affect our health.

It is best to keep our conversations positive. Good news brings health to our bones, so let's talk that good stuff. Stay away from negative conversation as much as possible. Smile to yourself and smile at others, as these small acts done in sincerity bring joy to our hearts. Amen!

Additional Inspiration: Psalm 52:9

Rx: Today be better than you were yesterday and tomorrow better than you are today. ~Dr. J

November 16

Proverb 16:32
Control

More than ever before it seems that we are living in a time that requires an exorbitant amount of patience. The increased use of high-speed, rapidly changing technology further exacerbates our desire for processes, procedures, and transactions to occur instantaneously. Now is almost too late! This technologically savvy modern-day society has managed to balance itself right on the edge of losing it.

In increasingly rare instances we experience extreme consequences of someone losing their patience and taking on a city. We have seen more violent terrorist acts over the past years due to people flat-out losing their mental grip. We have also seen more destroyed relationships and lack of love in our homes and communities. Nothing good comes when we are out of control and angry.

If you have lost your cool and said or done something to offend another, pray for better self-control and make amends with the person, if possible. If you have been the victim, pray for your offender. God loves us and wants peace for us. Shalom!

Additional Inspiration: Psalm 4:4–5

Rx: Today be better than you were yesterday and tomorrow better than you are today. ~Dr. J

November 17

Proverb 17:27
Restraint

Most of us can attest to putting our foot in our mouth one or two too many times. It sucks when we say something that we don't need to or tell a little too much of our perspective on an issue. It's even worse when we lose our cool or our ability to think straight. Think about the type of person you want to be. Being knowledgeable and understanding are definitely quality traits. If we can begin to see ourselves as having these attributes, then we can practice this Proverb with a little more ease. Go in peace!

Additional Inspiration: Psalm 19:14

November 18

Proverb 18:21
Life

You are what you speak! God used His powerful voice to speak life into order and to set boundaries within our universe. God spoke and things happened. He integrated all that we see and know. We humans, being made in His image, have the power to speak and things happen. According to Yahweh, our tongue, although one of the smallest parts of our body, has the most power.

Armed with the ability to energize and encourage or to insult and discourage, it is true that sticks and stones may break my bones and words *can* hurt you. The old saying may be cute for kids, but it is not reality. Words are powerful and can build us up or tear us down. Let's make a conscious effort to be mindful of the way we speak. Slow down and think. Ask Yah to make His thoughts yours and His ways your own. Press on!

Additional Inspiration: Psalm 117:1–2

Rx: Today be better than you were yesterday and tomorrow better than you are today. ~Dr. J

November 19

Proverb 19:23
Fear

When the Scriptures speak of fearing the Lord, we must understand this is a healthy fear and a reverent fear, similar to the honor and respect many of us had and still have for our earthly parents. If you are a parent, you recognize that you want that even with your own children. When we have a healthy fear of the Lord, we desire to please Him and not grieve Him.

This allows us to make better decisions, which leads to prosperity. We may still endure hard times and trouble may come our way, but Yahweh promises that we will remain unharmed and untouched, meaning trouble will not overtake us. Today, pray, ask, and thank God for a reverent fearing heart and mind. Amen!

Additional Inspiration: Psalm 31:19

November 20

Proverb 20:24
Understand

Do you ever have moments where you look back over your life and wonder how you got to where you are now? Of course you were conscious for the journey, but you find yourself playing a game of connect the dots as you reflect in retrospect about how one decision led to another. This is life! As we seek to know our way and plan every detail of our life, we truly have only a portion of control over how things turn out.

This is both exciting and scary, and we all respond differently at different times to this reality. We can understand as much about our future as God will reveal to us. With the remainder being unknown, our faith can help us overcome doubt, fear, and uncertainty. God is for us! He has plans to prosper us and not to harm us. I think we are safe following His lead, don't you? Amen!

Additional Inspiration: Psalm 27:8

Rx: Today be better than you were yesterday and tomorrow better than you are today. ~Dr. J

November 21

Proverb 21:30
Insight

We serve an all-knowing, omniscient God. Before we were, He was and will always be. All knowledge and wisdom and insight come from Him. He is the ultimate source of truth extending beyond the universe, and there is no worldly philosophy or ideology that can overpower Yahweh. That is how big our God is!

Anything our heart, mind, or spirit desires, we should approach Yah in confidence in prayer and sincerely ask Him for guidance. Ask for education and to surround you with Godly counsel and advisers. When we see decisions, laws, and policies made by leaders of the world that don't seem humanistic or for the benefit of the greater good, don't fret. When we see each injustice we must believe God's got it! Shalom.

Additional Inspiration: Psalm 119:91

November 22

Proverb 22:26-27
Pledge

Let's make a deal, or not. Yah gives very clear instruction to be cautious in making deals with people and the importance of paying debts. Every time we use debt or collateral, we are in essence "striking hands in pledge." We have heard stories of liens, wage garnishment, and in the worst case, bankruptcy. If you can't pay for what you want, you probably don't need it. If you can't pay for what you need, it is wise to ask for help, but be leery of the debt trap. There are always consequences when you owe others. Be blessed!

Additional Inspiration: Psalm 49:5-9

November 23

Proverb 23:26
Keep

Isn't it comforting to think that Yahweh wants our heart? He actually wants to be intimate with us. He didn't create us and abandon us. He created us and then made us an offer to dwell within us. Have you ever wished you had a trait of one of your siblings or someone famous? Ever heard someone say, "I wish I had a little bit of that or them inside of me"? The thought is that if you had that "thing," you would look better, perform better, think better, and so on.

The good news is that God is able to do this for each of us. When our heart is devoted to Him and our eyes keep focused on The Way, He operates on the inside of us to help us achieve the goals that He has set before us. What an amazing God we serve! Be blessed.

Additional Inspiration: Psalm 119:29–30

November 24

Proverb 24:28-29
Testify

Being misled, betrayed, taken advantage of, disrespected, and deceived are some of the worst experiences we go through as humans. When someone returns our kindness with evil or our meekness with greed, it hurts and can leave chronic wounds. We have been the victim or the offender or both at times in our lives. Many of us have ended up in court and wrapped up in lawsuits because of these situations. What God wants us to understand is the motive or inclination of the heart.

Testifying against someone without cause can happen in a work breakroom with staff gossip or in a courtroom between friends and ex-lovers. We easily use our lips to deceive in subtle ways. Yah wants us to be aware of this and change our behavior. He also wants to be our avenger so we don't need the motive of paying back evil with evil. As hard as it is, we must get this down so we can live healthy and blessed lives. Live wise!

Additional Inspiration: Psalm 119:84–86

Rx: Today be better than you were yesterday and tomorrow better than you are today. ~Dr. J

November 25

Proverb 25:26
Polluted

Everything about springs and freshwater wells sounds natural and refreshing. Many of us take getaways to places that have freshwater springs as a way to retreat and restore wellness. These are the places we go to remove ourselves of toxicity and heaviness. It is an interesting comparison to make between the freshest of pure waters and human beings. Yahweh uniquely illustrates that we, as the righteousness of Christ, are pure just like that delicious well water.

Only when we intentionally allow ourselves to be polluted by associating with people, places, activities, and thoughts that are toxic and unhealthy are we then muddied and polluted. Take time to consider this and pray for God's continual transformation in your life via the daily renewal of your mind. The only way is with Yahweh. Selah!

Additional Inspiration: Psalm 17:4–6

Rx: Today be better than you were yesterday and tomorrow better than you are today. ~Dr. J

November 26

Proverb 26:22
Inmost

We live in a society that is captivated by gossip. Much of our entertainment industry subsists on it, as we can't wait to hear the latest dish about people we don't know. This is further magnified in our personal relationships with people we know or may be acquainted with. There is something tempting about knowing information regarding others' lives.

Whether we know it to be true or not, it excites us. It is impossible to control everything we see and hear; media is all around us and in the palm of our hand. What we can control is what we say and how much we participate. Hold your tongue, turn the channel, politely excuse yourself from the conversation; we have a choice. Know your limits and be mindful.

Additional Inspiration: Psalm 55:12–14

Rx: Today be better than you were yesterday and tomorrow better than you are today. ~Dr. J

November 27

Proverb 27:21
Crucible

A crucible and furnace are used to test purity and to refine precious metals, such as silver and gold. In a similar way, Yahweh tests us to purify and refine us. One way God does this is through praise, such as in someone giving you a compliment or you winning an award. Remember to remain humble in your spirit and not let it go to your head of flesh. When we practice humility we will pass this test every time. Praise Jah!

Additional Inspiration: Psalm 57:9–10

November 28

Proverb 28:26
Trusts

As harsh as this sounds, it is real truth. We must get over ourselves! Yes, we have been fearfully and wonderfully made. Yes, we are all awesome creations. But we are not the Creator. We can't predict any of our life events or encounters with 100 percent certainty. God is merely suggesting that we practice humility and come to Him with all our plans and concerns. This is what it means to be wise and to practice wisdom. Pray about everything and ask God to show you direction. He loves us, protects us, and has a plan to prosper us. Yahweh is our safety zone! Shalom.

Additional Inspiration: Psalm 90:12

Rx: Today be better than you were yesterday and tomorrow better than you are today. ~Dr. J

November 29

Proverb 29:23
Pride

Dear friends, I know how much we want to avoid the low places in life. We want to stay riding the high tides and never face trials. There is nothing wrong with desiring perfection. God desired it for us, too. However, in this world, we will indeed face trouble. One area of trouble is our pride. When we are full of pride, we get a false sense of self and self-evaluation, a pseudo-high. Oftentimes this illusionary moment runs its course and reality brings us back to our senses. Sometimes this happens through losing something that we had been idolizing. Hence we get brought low.

When our spirits are in this lowly posture and we choose, in faith, to turn to Yahweh for strength and provision, we show Him that we have the right attitude toward our situation. These faith steps allow God to work through us, and so honoring us, as we glorify Him. This is a divine connection that God makes with those who love Him. Pray for God to cleanse us daily of pride and arrogance and to keep in us a humble spirit. Shalom!

Additional Inspiration: Psalm 116:15–16

November 30

Proverb 30:28
Dare

Dare to be bold! Dear Friends, who knew so much wisdom could be found in a sentence about lizard life? LOL! Only an omniscient God can show us how wisdom abounds from the least to the greatest in creation. Daring to step into places where you aren't qualified or familiar with sounds scary for some of us and adventurous for others.

The lizard having the audacity to set foot in the king's palace, a place so pristine and classy, knowing it can easily get swept out, stepped on, or caught by bare hands, demonstrates the concept of being bold and daring. The lizards live on the edge! Let's dare to live on the edge of "yikes" like the lizard and conquer our fears—obviously respecting our safety, but taking a leap of faith to be bold, take chances, and go where we might never dare to adventure. Remember, Yahweh says the lizards are extremely wise. Amen!

Additional Inspiration: Psalm 34:4–5

Rx: Today be better than you were yesterday and tomorrow better than you are today. ~Dr. J

DECEMBER

Even a fool is thought wise if he keeps silent, and discerning if he holds his tongue.

Proverb 17:28

December 1

Proverb 1:33
Ease

Healthy, obedient, well-mannered children are the desire of every caring parent. They believe children who will listen and value their advice and instructions will live in safety and be at ease without fear of harm. This belief is easy to defend when it comes to children, but as adults we still need and have accountability. Our heavenly father, Jehovah, desires the same for us. Today, let us focus on aligning ourselves with this request from Yah. Then watch God's blessings of peace fall upon us. Amen!

Additional Inspiration: Psalm 119:44

December 2

Proverb 2:22
Unfaithful

We cannot live how we want, with no respect or reverence for God, His laws, and His creation, which includes other humans, and expect to be unscathed. Can man walk on hot coals and not be burned? (Proverb 6:28) Of course not! Not in the natural anyway. We reap what we sow, and although it may not always appear that way in society, looks can be deceiving.

If we believe Yah is who He says He is, then we know He is a just and fair God. He created both the weight and the scales, and dishonesty is detestable to Him. We will all give an account, so let's concentrate on our personal transformation, our unique mission, and running our race with integrity and love. Be blessed!

Additional Inspiration: Psalm 10:12–15

Rx: Today be better than you were yesterday and tomorrow better than you are today. ~Dr. J

December 3

Proverb 3:30
Accuse

Verse from Psalms: "It to mine to avenge." If you have ever been falsely accused, you know the feeling of wanting to defend yourself and plead your case. Many of us deal with this in our homes, in our workplace, and in our friendships. It can lead to feelings of betrayal, bitterness, resentment, and self-pity. When this arises, we must pray and remember Yahweh is our avenger.

Pray with the boldness as David did, and declare victory over your life. Although hard, forgive and extend mercy as Yah has on you. If you have been on the other side, the one falsely accusing others, take time to repair that relationship. Apologize to the one you offended. God will remove the sting of the offense and give you peace. Trust and believe Him for it. Amen!

Additional Inspiration: Psalm 118:6–7

December 4

Proverb 4:25-26
Swerve

If you have ever experienced driving in a new city where there was a lot to see as you drove by, after swerving once or twice, you quickly realize that it is very dangerous to look excessively for too long at any one thing, because you could very easily crash. Your eyes must remain fixed ahead on the road and other drivers in front of, behind, and alongside of you. No doubt most of us probably prefer riding and driving on smooth pavement rather than a bumpy road, as the latter demands a heightened level of attention. Similarly, in life management we must not get too distracted by the multi-stimulus packages that surround us.

The temptations, the lures, and the "too much of a good thing" can easily derail us off that smooth course onto the bumpy road that is so unpleasant. For those of us into off-roading, that's another thing. Continue to pray for His specific guidance and direction. He is our firm foundation and will never be shaken. Shalom!

Additional Inspiration: Psalm 119:133

Rx: Today be better than you were yesterday and tomorrow better than you are today. ~Dr. J

December 5

Proverb 5:23
Astray

Unfortunately this is a real truth that numerous people face daily. Many of the common diseases killing us are self-inflicted by the choices we make. We want to enjoy everything that we desire and without moderation. We make poor food choices, smoke, drink excessively, gamble, steal, overspend, and don't exercise enough.

When we are not willing to do what is right, we will get sick, mentally, spiritually, and physically. We will be positively rewarded when we make better life choices and live more disciplined. Just try it and see. You have nothing to lose and everything good to gain. Shalom!

Additional Inspiration: Psalm 49:13–14

December 6

Proverb 6:32
Judgment

To be in any position lacking judgment can be scary and dangerous. Our decisions affect not only us, but the other people directly and indirectly involved. No matter how you try to view it, adultery brings grief and sorrow to the majority involved. Like a drug that gives a short-lived high where you feel so happy and free, so it is with an adulterous affair.

After the excitement wears off and reality sets in, after the kids, coworkers, family, and spouses find out, the fun is over and the pain often begins. Relationships are broken because trust was forsaken and emptiness remains. We easily destroy ourselves and others. Run from the temptation of adultery and encourage others to do the same. Pray for those who are trapped in it. Wisdom speaks!

Additional Inspiration: Psalm 25:21

Rx: Today be better than you were yesterday and tomorrow better than you are today. ~Dr. J

December 7

Proverb 7:27
Death

No doubt, we are going to die; that is a fact. Another fact is that we can usher in an untimely death experience by the choices we make. This is the concept contained within this Proverb. The list of ill ways we can choose to behave is long. Our actions, choices, thoughts, and words have consequences. Many diseases that we face are preventable with proper diet, exercising, and hygiene habits.

This is perplexing because we can spend so much money on healthcare quick fixes but rarely spend the mental and physical energy to implement the changes needed for lifetime success. The more we train ourselves to walk in an elevated level of spiritual awareness, the healthier we will be. Trust and believe it. Shalom!

Additional Inspiration: Psalm 40:8

December 8

Proverb 8:35-36
Favor

Hallelujah! Yahweh has made known to us the way to receive His favor and to find life. For a moment, consider how often Proverbs instruct us to find wisdom. The fact that there are chapters dedicated to this topic is telling of the importance. No one wants to be lost in this life. We all benefit from the Lord's favor. Let's continue to seek out wisdom so we can live in the abundant blessing Jesus promises us.

It is clear that living an unwise life leads to mental, physical, and spiritual harm and possible separation from God if you have not accepted Jesus as your Lord and savior. If you are saved, of course you will never be cut off from God, but you will miss out on the enriched life He has planned for you. Press and be blessed!

Additional Inspiration: Psalm 37:4

Rx: Today be better than you were yesterday and tomorrow better than you are today. ~Dr. J

December 9

Proverb 9:18
Foolish

This verse is very chilling in its description of the consequences of partnering with the foolish ways of the world. We are in a state of social decay, and there will one day be a final restoration! Until then, we are trying to manage an inflammatory situation with temporary agents. Dear friend, can we not agree that life is already hard as it is? Can we agree that we don't need to look for trouble to bring on ourselves? As you read the Proverbs, remember Yahweh is giving us freedom of choice, but He is pleading with us to choose wisely to avoid unwanted harm. Selah!

Additional Inspiration: Psalm 140:4–5

December 10

Proverb 10:26
Sluggard

Vinegar is acidic and will dissolve teeth, and smoke burns the eyes. Both are harsh irritants that decrease dependability and limit proper usage for eating and seeing. What an interesting choice of comparison for God to use. Yahweh describes the sluggard and lazy people as undependable. Their lack of desire to be active brings negative consequences to them and to those dependent on them. Work brings purpose to our life. It is in our best interest to not be lazy and to avoid relying on lazy people to get any job done. Shalom!

Additional Inspiration: Psalm 62:11–12

December 11

Proverb 11:30
Win

We all have the ability to speak life into one another and to win souls. It is so easy for us to think this is the job of a pastor or other church staff, but it's actually the great commission that has been given to us all. Jesus instructs us to go to the ends of the earth sharing the good news of the gospel. In a nutshell, we have all sinned and fallen short of the glory of God. The ultimate punishment for our sins is death. BUT...Jesus died for our sins!

He rose again from death to give us new life and eternity with Yahweh. When we share our testimony, when we encourage one another, when we bear good fruit and spread spiritual seed, we become a tree of life to another human being. Trust and believe this makes our God smile. These are the actions of soul winners. Win and be blessed!

Additional Inspiration: Psalm 11:30

December 12

Proverb 12:26
Cautious

Many parents are overly cautious about who their children spend time with. Many parents interview other parents prior to trips or sleepovers, and rightfully so, because bad company corrupts good character. Our spiritual parent, El Shaddai expects us all to adhere to this same guidance. Adults oddly enough appear to be just as susceptible to peer pressure as kids are. The downside is that as an adult, the consequences can be more severe and long term. Life is a series of choices, and the good ones will lead to a harvest. This is God's promise. Amen!

Additional Inspiration: Psalm 38:19–20

December 13

Proverb 13:23
Injustice

When we hear of starving children in certain countries or see them on a TV broadcast, it breaks our hearts. It also leads to the question: why are there so many food shortages around the world? Well, this Proverb tells quite plainly that one of the reasons for food shortages is manmade injustice. The fact that this was observed and written about from so long ago should leave us less surprised that it happens now. We should feel more compelled to make a difference any way that we can and seek to restore and maintain justice. One way we do this is by donating our time, talent, and resources to bless others. Shalom!

Additional Inspiration: Psalm 14:6

December 14

Proverb 14:33
Reposes

If we want to be wise and make better decisions, we simply have to ask Yahweh for it. The Holy Spirit (T.H.S.) was sent to us by God to be our personal guidance counselor. T.H.S., much like our G.P.S., contains all the wisdom, discernment, knowledge, and understanding we need to get us to our destination at any time. We don't have to worry about system crashes or lack of signal with T.H.S.

Wisdom does not wish to elude us. Wisdom actually wants to be known by us. Fancy this idea for a moment! This is both fantastic in thought and protective in the physical sense. She is here to guide us and keep us from harm. To those who seek her, she shows up in many forms, appeals to many senses, and reposes to communicate with us.

She even speaks to us in advance when we are foolish at heart and on the brink of making poor decisions. We have been given a beautiful opportunity from God to live right. Exercise your relationship with wisdom. She's got your back 24/7. Shalom!

Additional Inspiration: Psalm 73:23–24

Rx: Today be better than you were yesterday and tomorrow better than you are today. ~Dr. J

December 15

Proverb 15:32
Discipline

Suicide has been steadily rising in the United States. When we despise ourselves, we have lost love for our own life, our own humanity. This is an ultimate tragedy to a beautifully created being. Many of us have felt the desire to end our life but we never took that step, thankfully. Fortunately, others have never considered it.

This Proverb wants us for a moment to consider that although we may be here physically, we can commit spiritual suicide by not harnessing our full God-given potential. When we don't like discipline and resist from turning from our evil ways and unhealthy habits, we hold ourselves back from becoming our best. Some of us flat out never attain our goals. We don't want to hear correction or walk in the ways of understanding because we actually despise our own selves.

Think about it for a minute. It is ironic because we live in a culture that encourages us to confess how much we love ourselves through selfies and "i-everything." Do we really feel that way? Let's commit to realigning our life in a way that represents our true love of God. Listen for Him prompting your Spirit in the areas where you need to change. Let the transformation begin!

Additional Inspiration: Psalm 119:70–71

Rx: Today be better than you were yesterday and tomorrow better than you are today. ~Dr. J

December 16

Proverb 16:33
Lot

Your beginning doesn't determine your future; it is all in the Lord's hands. Thank Yah for that promise. This is the only way to explain how many people have survived such horrific beginnings, later to share with the world how they triumphed over tragedy. The lot is cast and we are born into the family we are born into. This is out of our control, as far as we know.

The decisions our parents make are certainly out of our control and can affect our lives forever, both good and bad. However, the Creator of the universe understands what we face, and when we align our lives with Him, He can and will make insurmountable circumstances dissipate. Where there is an obstacle or hurdle, He will allow us to go through, over, and around it.

Yahweh wants good for us, and He works everything for the good of those who love Him. Don't worry or be embarrassed or ashamed about where you came from. In fact thank Him for it! Fix your eyes on Him. Get excited about where you are now while looking forward to where you are going. Be brave!

Additional Inspiration: Psalm 16:5

Rx: Today be better than you were yesterday and tomorrow better than you are today. ~Dr. J

December 17

Proverb 17:28
Discerning

We must learn the art of knowing when and where to speak up and to shut up. It is very clear instruction throughout the Proverbs that we do not have freedom of speech as our American Constitution so declares. According to Yahweh, only a fool speaks everything and anything that comes to mind. We must exercise total self-control with our words.

Yes, sometimes it is actually better to not say anything at all. As you begin to practice this, you will experience a different sense of liberty and begin to realize that everything doesn't need to be said. This is a powerful way to live. Let's think! Be blessed!

Additional Inspiration: Psalm 34:11–14

December 18

Proverb 18:24
Friend

We live in a modern, tech-savvy world where some people boast millions, thousands, and hundreds of followers and friends. Yet we are experiencing an increase in loneliness and the number of suicides. Social media networks are great on so many levels, but nothing can replace the experience of real true love and friendship.

As this Proverb indicates, we may find close friendships with blood relatives or those unrelated to us. No matter what, we have an ultimate friendship with Jesus who lives in our heart. Don't feel bad if you don't have an entourage; just focus on creating loving, meaningful relationships with a few, and especially with God. Shalom!

Additional Inspiration: Psalm 119:8–9

December 19

Proverb 19:24
Sluggard

This is a degree of laziness that some of us may never fully understand, but if it didn't exist, Yahweh wouldn't have written about it. Amen if this doesn't describe you, but something can still be learned from this verse. Laziness is not favorable with God, and He actually rewards hard work. Our works, of course, do not save us, but our deeds do have merit.

God promises that each of us will give an account for our life at the Day of Judgment. If you are a person who lives life with a purpose, then it is evident in the actions you take to fulfill that purpose. None of this can be achieved if we are sluggardly. Enjoy your Sabbath and take time for rest, but let's do like the Holy Spirit and keep it flowing. Amen!

Additional Inspiration: Psalm 119:168

December 20

Proverb 20:25
Rashly

Be careful making commitments. We are in a time when many of us are overachieving, overcommitting, overscheduling, and in over our heads. We have to be very cautious with our "yes" and what we agree to, especially when our decisions affect other people. When we act first and think second, we easily find ourselves in situations we don't really want to be in. Always pray about a situation prior to engaging. Ask God to surround you with the right people and guide you in making right choices. Be blessed!

Additional Inspiration: Psalm 25:4

December 21

Proverb 21:31
Victory

We can prepare ourselves, condition, and practice, but we ultimately cannot predict with 100 percent certainty (given we are not in a rigged system) the winner of any said competition. Likewise, we can't predict what time we will cross the finish line of our race, because we cannot see what lies ahead. We don't know what may allow us to finish faster or what may slow us down, but there is one who knows, and that is our omniscient God, El Shaddai Adonai. Hallelujah that our victory rests with Him, no matter what day or time. Therefore, it is wise to be ready, stay ready, and wait patiently on the Lord. Shalom!

Additional Inspiration: Psalm 60:11–12

December 22

Proverb 22:29
Skilled

Jehovah has given each of us a unique assignment, a skill, talent, and trade handcrafted by Him. When God made us in His image, He made us with personality, an ability to learn, and ability to love. Each of us has a responsibility to nurture our gifts, talents, and skills. This falls under the category of good stewardship.

We should strive for excellence in our work, no matter what we do for a living. Because we reap what we sow, we should be mindful to sow into our daily work. God promises that our commitment to mastering our gifts will be noticed by others and be well rewarded. Amen!

Additional Inspiration: Psalm 22:29

Rx: Today be better than you were yesterday and tomorrow better than you are today. ~Dr. J

December 23

Proverb 23:29-35
Sorrow

Take extra time to pray for those who deal with alcoholism, substance abuse, or other addictive behaviors. This describes in a few short sentences the lifestyle of a person trapped in the cycle of addiction. We can pray freedom for those we know personally and for people across the entire world that face this trap daily. If you are struggling with addiction, know that I am personally praying for you, even though I don't know your name. Yahweh, we pray you rain down your power that breaks every chain that binds us. Amen!

Additional Inspiration: Psalm 13:1-4

December 24

Proverb 24:30–34
Sluggard

Many of us have had those days, weeks or months, or even years when we just couldn't bring ourselves to get motivated for projects, tasks, outings, and so on. Sometimes it is easy to go to work and to do the "work thing" because we have a boss or someone holding us accountable. Our paycheck is also a strong motivator.

When we get off work, that same level of accountability no longer exists, and we must become fully self-propelled. Lack of drive, desire, and hustle is a curse of the sluggard. Remember that when we care for what we have and respond to God's calling on our life, we actually honor Him. This does require work on our part. Shalom!

Additional Inspiration: Psalm 130:1–4

Rx: Today be better than you were yesterday and tomorrow better than you are today. ~Dr. J

December 25

Proverb 25:28
Self-Control

A city whose walls are broken down is a city that is unsafe and open to anything. This is a dangerous position for the inhabitants as it leaves them susceptible to attack, devastation, and ultimately death. Well, Yahweh compares this to a person who lacks self-control. Prudence is our wall, our soul's fortress. Self-control can keep us from making wrong decisions, thus protecting our inner man. Without it we are fools left to our own folly and are open for attack. Not a good look. Let's think. Amen!

Additional Inspiration: Psalm 86:5–7

December 26

Proverb 26:24–25
Abominations

If you have ever experienced being verbally deceived, you understand the power of this Proverb. This is an example of the expression, "a wolf in sheep's clothing." Most of us naturally want to trust and believe people. It feels easier to take someone at face value, yet this verse clearly illustrates we cannot always make the assumption that someone is trustworthy or has our best interest at heart.

So, how do we know when we have encountered someone who fits this description of deception, especially if they disguise it so well? Yah encourages us to exercise restraint before engaging in any relationship or business deal. Friends, we have to do our research. Pray, Google, and let God guide. Amen!

Additional Inspiration: Psalm 55:20–21

Rx: Today be better than you were yesterday and tomorrow better than you are today. ~Dr. J

December 27

Proverb 27:23-24
Steward

Nothing is a guarantee, except the truth and salvation of God's Word and the work of Jesus. God gives all of us the same charge, to be good stewards over the things that He has given us: time, talent, and treasure. Each one of us has a spiritual accountant responsibility. When we aren't aware of the condition of our health, finances, children, relationships, or business, anything can and will happen, even losing it all.

Ever spent too much money and wondered how it happened? Or what about time? Ever wasted so much of your day only to wonder, "Where did the time go?" It's easy to lose track, especially in today's fast-paced society. Ask God to point you to wise counsel and to help you step up your stewardship game. Pray and practice!

Additional Inspiration: Psalm 73:27-28

Rx: Today be better than you were yesterday and tomorrow better than you are today. ~Dr. J

December 28

Proverb 28:27
Poor

Does this verse make you want to go out immediately and give? I will pass on the curses, Lord, thank you! Many major, overly crowded urban cities are full of people who are down on their luck, transient, and poor in finances and spirit. Oftentimes we drive past them and think, "I should have given" or "Someone else will help them."

When we consider that we are that "someone else," we will begin to change others' lives as well as our own. We cannot give to every single person, but we do have a responsibility to help those that God places on our hearts to help. Stay sensitive to Yah's promptings of your spirit, and next time you hear Him whisper to you, give—don't think twice, just do it! Shalom.

Additional Inspiration: Psalm 112:9

December 29

Proverb 29:25
Snare

It is so easy for us to get caught up in the web of people-pleasing and people-fearing. We are often worried we won't be liked or well-received, worried we won't get the promotion or our secrets will be leaked. We live in a state where we feel we are at the mercy of other people rather than the mercy of our Creator, El Shaddai. To some degree, we are at the mercy of one another, and we must learn to trust each other in times that may be difficult or stressful.

We must always remember that if God is for us, who can be against us? What can mere man do? When we come up against trying circumstances or situations where we may dishonor Yahweh in order to please man, we must immediately stop and pray. We should never have to compromise doing what is right for fear that we will lose our job, marriage, mind, or salvation. Think twice and put your trust in Yah's way. He will always protect us and keep us safe. Selah!

Additional Inspiration: Psalm 112:7

Rx: Today be better than you were yesterday and tomorrow better than you are today. ~Dr. J

December 30

Proverb 30:33
Strife

We are emotional creatures. God designed us with these qualities, and they serve a meaningful purpose in our life. Our emotions are nothing to be ashamed of. Like most things in our realm, too much is *no bueno* (no good). Even Proverbs states when we eat too much honey, we will vomit. And so it is with our emotions. When we let anger get out of control and we stir it up within ourselves, and the relationships around us, we become a composer of tense, unbearable, loathsome situations.

When you see the production of strife for what it is, you realize you don't want that lifestyle. So let's all pray today that we keep our anger in check and directed at appropriate parties, the enemy Satan, and the injustice that exists. Praise God that He is going to have the final word. Amen!

Additional Inspiration: Psalm 116:7

Rx: Today be better than you were yesterday and tomorrow better than you are today. ~Dr. J

December 31

Proverb 31:31
Reward

Yahweh promises us earned rewards for our works. Our rewards are a reflection of what we sow. The woman of Proverb 31 is of noble character because she chooses righteousness and productivity. Jah not only has a reward for us, but He also has praises awaiting us from the community of lives that we serve. Ask God to show you your purposes and then get busy working it out. When we are obedient to our calling, which happens through a healthy fear of the Lord, we are sowing seed for the reward we will one day reap. Selah!

Additional Inspiration: Psalm 117:1–2

Glossary

Abba: Father
Adonai: Master owner, Majesty
Amen: So be it

El Shaddai: God Almighty, Supply, Comfort, Power
El Elyon: The most high God, Strength, Sovereign, Supreme
Elohim: Strong one, Sovereign God, Creative

Jah: Short for Jehovah and variation of Yah
Jehovah: Personal Hebrew name for God. The Supreme God
Jehovah Jireh (Yireh): The Lord will provide, Provision
Jehovah Rappha: The Lord who heals, Healer

Proverb: Wisdom for action
Psalm: Song

Selah: Unknown but thought to mean "Stop and listen", "Stop and think", a musical break, "Pause to weigh the meaning", or "Measure or weigh in balances".
Shalom: Peace

Yahweh (YWHW): Hebrew name for God, I am that I am, To exist, To be, Self-existent God
Yeshua: Hebrew for Jesus, Salvation

SWA:REI™

This is a SWA:REI product.

Live Your Life Inspired!
We create art, music, apparel, and books that encourage, nourish, and refine the mind and soul.

Be on the look out for more products that inspire coming soon!

About The Author

Dr. Malieka Johnson is a General and Adult Special Needs Dentist who considers herself a healer, artist and humanitarian. She is the master of the jack-of-all-trades and having a wide range of interests has allowed her to acquire a unique set of skills, talents, and abilities. Dr. Johnson has a degree in psychology from University of California, San Diego (UCSD) and earned a Doctor of Dental Surgery degree from University of California, Los Angeles (UCLA). In May 2018, Dr. Johnson was recognized as a, Top 40 dentist under 40 years old by Incisal Edge Magazine for her pioneering work with adults with special needs, leadership, and her consistent humanitarian outreach.

Dr. Johnson has complimented her education by completing multiple leadership programs and earning a certification in personal training. She is an artist, musician, philanthropist, and actively volunteers in her community, church, and on multiple non-profit boards. She is also the founder of the inspirational company, SWA:REI and The Humanitarian and Education Relief Operation (H.E.R.O.) Project, a non-profit that focuses on leadership education and scholarships for underrepresented professionals. Learn more at ourheroproject.org.

Visit Dr. Johnson's website
www.maliekajohnson.com

CPSIA information can be obtained
at www.ICGtesting.com
Printed in the USA
FSHW010046290519
58499FS